Tormented in Hades

Tormented in Hades

The Rich Man and Lazarus (Luke 16:19–31) and Other Lucan Parables for Persuading the Rich to Repentance

JOHN A. SZUKALSKI

☙PICKWICK *Publications* • Eugene, Oregon

TORMENTED IN HADES
The Rich Man and Lazarus (Luke 16:19–31) and Other Lucan Parables for Persuading the Rich to Repentance

Copyright © 2013 John A. Szukalski. All rights reserved. Except for brief quotations in critical publications or reviews, no part of this book may be reproduced in any manner without prior written permission from the publisher. Write: Permissions, Wipf and Stock Publishers, 199 W. 8th Ave., Suite 3, Eugene, OR 97401.

Unless otherwise noted, Scripture texts in this work are taken from the *New American Bible, revised edition* © 2010, 1991, 1986, 1970 Confraternity of Christian Doctrine, Washington, D.C. and are used by permission of the copyright owner. All Rights Reserved. No part of the New American Bible may be reproduced in any form without permission in writing from the copyright owner.

Pickwick Publications
An Imprint of Wipf and Stock Publishers
199 W. 8th Ave., Suite 3
Eugene, OR 97401

www.wipfandstock.com

ISBN 13: 978-1-62032-390-8

Cataloguing-in-Publication data:

Szukalski, John A.

Tormented in hades: the rich man and Lazarus (Luke 16:19–31) and other Lucan parables for persuading the rich to repentance / John A. Szukalski

xii + 170 pp. ; 23 cm. Includes bibliographical references and index.

ISBN 13: 978-1-62032-390-8

1. Rich man and Lazarus (Parable). 2. Bible, Luke—Criticism, interpretation, etc. 3. Wealth—Biblical teaching. 4. Poor—Biblical teaching. I. Title.

BS2545 S996 2013

Manufactured in the U.S.A.

To my father and mother, John T. and Anna Szukalski, on the occasion of their forty-seventh wedding anniversary, June 4, 2013

May the darkness of sin and the night of unbelief,
Vanish before the light of the Word and the spirit of Grace;
And may the heart of Jesus
Live in the hearts of all. Amen.

—Saint Arnold Janssen

Contents

Preface | ix
Abbreviations | xi

1. Modern Research on the Parable of the Rich Man and Lazarus (Luke 16:19–31) | 1
2. The Parable of the Rich Man and Lazarus and the Lucan Travel Narrative Parables for the Repentance of the Rich | 39
3. Socio-Narratological Analysis of Selected Lucan Travel Narrative Parables and Selected Works from Lucian of Samosata | 74
4. Socio-Narratological Exegesis of the Parable of the Rich Man and Lazarus (Luke 16:19–31) | 119
5. Conclusion: Rhetorical Strategy of Persuading the Rich to Repent in the Φιλάργυροι Parables of the Lucan Travel Narrative | 148

Bibliography | 159
Index of Scripture Citations | 165

Preface

THE PARABLE OF THE Rich Man and Lazarus should make us very uncomfortable. On the face of it, the parable depicts a rich man who enjoys full use of his wealth to live quite comfortably, while the poor man is depicted as barely clinging to life and wholly dependent upon others for his welfare. The assumption is that the rich man's wealth is his own, earned through hard work and an entrepreneurial spirit, while the poor man's poverty must be the result of sloth and lack of industry. This is just the way things are, aren't they? The problem is that the parable seems to condemn the rich man to torments in Hades for no other apparent reason than his wealth and to reward poor Lazarus with bliss at Abraham's side for no other apparent reason than his poverty. Is divine judgment simply a matter of eternal reward for the poor and condemnation for the rich, a mathematical function inversely proportional to one's financial net worth? Such an amoral and mechanical criterion of judgment cannot be the criterion utilized by the personal and loving God of Jesus Christ as presented to us in the Gospels, can it?

Or taken another way, is not the rich man's prosperity a tangible sign of divine blessing for a life well-lived, and the poor man's misery an obvious sign of a divine punishment for a life of moral bankruptcy? After all, many people instinctively judge their neighbors' economic, social, and medical well-being, or lack thereof, in just such a way. But if this were true, then why would God reverse the eternal fates of these men upon their deaths? That does not make sense either. So what's going on here?

The parable of the Rich Man and Lazarus in Luke 16:19–31 is one of seven Φιλάργυροι or "money-lover" parables in the Lucan Travel Narrative that evinces a rhetorical strategy of persuading the rich to repentance by utilizing parabolic dynamics that move the reader away from an established vision of reality that is exclusive and elitist toward an alternate vision of

Preface

reality that is inclusive, egalitarian, and associated with Jesus' preaching of the kingdom of God. These parables exhibit coherent profiles of the unrepentant rich who display stereotypical behaviors and attitudes that are antithetical to the alternative kingdom of God vision of reality, along with recurring and convergent social concerns that require transformation.

The parable of the Rich Man and Lazarus, when read utilizing the socio-narratological approach employed in this book, comes alive with new insights and implications for living a more authentic Christian discipleship—one that discredits the so-called "prosperity gospel" of wealth, health, and success based on the highly selective and erroneous reading of Scripture promoted by certain modern televangelists. The Lucan Jesus addresses the issue of whether it is possible to be both rich and Christian, and if so, what concrete actions rich Christians must perform to demonstrate true repentance and discipleship. Conversely, it demonstrates the ultimate fate of the unrepentant rich—to be tormented with the memory of their former wealth and honor, and to be permanently excluded from afterlife reward for their failure to obey the Law and the Prophets regarding their obligation to care for the poor. And this could make some people very uncomfortable indeed.

This book is a lightly revised version of my doctoral dissertation written at The Catholic University of America in Washington, DC. Special thanks to my dissertation director, Frank J. Matera, for his patient and generous guidance, along with my dissertation readers, John Paul Heil and Francis T. Gignac. I also want to acknowledge Thomas A. Krosnicki who proofread the final manuscript of this book and especially C. H. Nguyen for invaluable technical assistance and support.

January 15, 2013
Feast of St. Arnold Janssen

John A. Szukalski, SVD
Assistant Professor in Theology
Divine Word College
Epworth, Iowa

Abbreviations

AB	Anchor Bible
ABD	*Anchor Bible Dictionary.* Edited by D. N. Freedman. 6 vols. New York: Doubleday, 1992
AKPAW	Abhandlungen der königlich preussischen Akademie der Wissenschaften
ANTC	Abingdon New Testament Commentaries
BDAG	Bauer, W., F. W. Danker, W. F. Arndt, and F. W. Gingrich. *Greek-English Lexicon of the New Testament and Other Early Christian Literature.* 3d ed. Chicago: University of Chicago Press, 2000
BIS	Biblical Interpretation Series
BTB	*Biblical Theology Bulletin*
CBQ	*Catholic Biblical Quarterly*
ExpTim	*Expository Times*
Int	*Interpretation*
JBL	*Journal of Biblical Literature*
JSNT	*Journal for the Study of the New Testament*
JSNTSup	Journal for the Study of the New Testament: Supplement Series
JTS	*Journal of Theological Studies*
NIGTC	New International Greek Testament Commentary
NJBC	*The New Jerome Biblical Commentary.* Edited by R. E. Brown et al. Englewood Cliffs: Prentice Hall, 1990
NovT	*Novum Testamentum*
NovTSup	Supplements to Novum Testamentum
NTS	*New Testament Studies*
OBT	Overtures to Biblical Theology
PL	*Patrologia latina* [= Patrologiae cursus completus: Series latina]. Edited by J.-P. Migne. 217 vols. Paris: Migne, 1844–64

Abbreviations

REJ	*Revue des études juives*
RSR	*Recherches de science religieuse*
SBLDS	Society of Biblical Literature Dissertation Series
SBLMS	Society of Biblical Literature Monograph Series
SBLSP	*Society of Biblical Literature Seminar Papers*
Semeia	*Semeia*
SNTSMS	Society for New Testament Studies Monograph Series
SP	Sacra pagina
TS	*Theological Studies*
VT	*Vetus Testamentum*
WBC	Word Biblical Commentary

1

Modern Research on the Parable of the Rich Man and Lazarus (Luke 16:19–31)

THE PARABLE OF THE Rich Man and Lazarus in Luke 16:19–31 is unique and problematic. It is the only canonical parable referring to at least one character by a proper name and the only one portraying a scene in the afterlife. The permanent reversal of fortunes at death depicts the rich man in torment in Hades and the poor man in bliss in Abraham's bosom, a reversal that appears to be based solely upon their respective economic standings in life—a disturbing criterion of judgment. This uniqueness has occasioned divergent, even contradictory, conclusions with regard to the parable's literary and conceptual background, its unity and authenticity, and its function within the overall Lucan narrative.

Ancient commentary upon the parable presented a range of interpretive methods, from the literal to the allegorical. In late fourth-century Antioch, John Chrysostom (d. 407) preached a series of four vivid sermons in which he systematically interpreted the parable of the Rich Man and Lazarus with regard to the scandalous insensitivity and injustice of the prosperous rich toward the suffering poor:

> This cruelty is the worst kind of wickedness; it is an inhumanity without rival. For it is not the same thing for one who lives in poverty not to help those in need, as for one who enjoys luxury to neglect others who are wasting away with hunger. Again, it is not the same thing to see a poor man once or twice and pass him by, as to

> look at him every day and not be aroused by the persistent sight to mercy and generosity. Again, it is not the same thing for one who is troubled in his heart by misfortune and distress not to help his neighbor, as for one who enjoys such happiness and continuous good fortune to neglect others who are wasting away with hunger, to lock up his heart, and not to be made more generous by his own joy. For surely you know this, that even if we are the most savage of men, we usually are made more gentle and kindly by good fortune. But that man was not improved by his prosperity, but remained beastly, or rather he surpassed the cruelty and inhumanity of any beast in his behavior.[1]

In his preaching, Chrysostom sought to illustrate the literal meaning of the text along with the consequent moral exhortations for leading a virtuous Christian life. Such an approach is in line with his training in the Antiochene exegetical tradition, associated with his teacher Diodorus of Tarsus (d. 390) and fellow student Theodore of Mopsuestia (d. 428).

In contrast to such stark realism and social critique, the Alexandrian exegetical tradition associated with Clement of Alexandria (d. 215) and Origen (d. 254) emphasized an allegorical interpretation of Scripture that in extreme cases was presented as a key to the secret truths of the faith reserved for the initiated—a kind of Christian gnosis.[2] Such an allegorical interpretation of the parable of the Rich Man and Lazarus is exemplified in the writings of Augustine of Hippo (d. 430):

> We should take Lazarus to mean our Lord; lying at the gate of the rich man, because he condescended to the proud ears of the Jews in the lowliness of His incarnation; desiring to be fed from the crumbs which fell from the rich man's table, that is, seeking from them even the least works of righteousness.... The wounds are the

---

1. Roth, *St. John Chrysostom*, 22–23. Chrysostom's series of sermons treated the parable in four parts: Luke 16:19–21, where he argues that the rich man's self-indulgent life harmed his own spiritual health but Lazarus built up his spiritual strength through the patient endurance of suffering in poverty; vv. 22–24, where he asserts that the rich have positive duties toward the poor, regardless of the moral qualities of the one in need; vv. 24–26, where he asserts that whether one is rich or poor, one's deeds affect the condition of one's life after death; and vv. 27–31, where he discusses the incorruptible role of one's conscience in seeking repentance before the time of judgment and recompense after death. Roth includes two other sermons by Chrysostom on the topic of wealth and poverty not directly related to this parable.

2. Brown and Schneiders, "Hermeneutics," 1154–55. For a more complete comparison of the Alexandrian and Antiochene exegetical methods, see Guillet, "d'Alexandrie et d'Antioche," 257–302, and Burghardt, "Early Christian Exegesis," 78–116.

sufferings of our Lord, the dogs who licked them are the Gentiles, whom the Jews called unclean, and yet, with the sweetest odor of devotion, they lick the sufferings of our Lord in the Sacraments of His Body and Blood throughout the whole world. Abraham's bosom is understood to be the hiding place of the Father, whither after His Passion our Lord rising again was taken up, whither He was said to be carried by the angels, as it seems to me, because that reception by which Christ reached the Father's secret place the angels announced to the disciples.[3]

A degree of allegory was already evident in the interpretation of Jesus' parables as presented in the Synoptic Gospels, most notably in the parables of the Sower and the Seed (Mark 4:13–20) and the Weeds in the Wheat (Matt 13:36–43).[4] However, the more extensive and complex allegorization associated with the Alexandrian exegetical tradition came to dominate parabolic exegesis throughout the patristic and medieval eras, a dominance that persisted until the end of the nineteenth century with the 1889 publication of Adolf Jülicher's seminal work, *Die Gleichnisreden Jesu*.[5] Jülicher regarded allegory as a genre too sophisticated for a simple preacher from Galilee to utilize, especially when compared with the classical Greek works of Aristotle, and therefore rejected the validity of the allegorical interpretation of Gospel texts.[6] Rather, he asserted that the early church obscured the original parabolic message of Jesus through a process of allegorization, descriptive supplementation, and interpretive application. The original parables of Jesus were

---

3. Augustine alternately interprets the rich man as "the proud Jews ignorant of the righteousness of God," Lazarus as "some Gentile or Publican," the dogs as "those most wicked men who loved sin, who with a large tongue cease not to praise the evil works, which another loathes, groaning in himself, and confessing" and the rich man's five brothers as "the Jews who were called five, because they were bound under the Law, which was given by Moses who wrote five books." Augustini Hipponensis, "Quaestionum Evangeliorum," 1350–52. For other patristic and medieval allegorical interpretations of this and other parables, see Wailes, *Medieval Allegories*, 253–60.

4. Drury (*Parables in the Gospels*, 117) argues that in some cases allegory is intended, albeit implicit, as in the parable of the Prodigal Son in Luke 15:11–32: "The father stands for God, the older son is orthodox unreconstructed Judaism, and the prodigal who has put himself beyond the orthodox Jewish pale by his fornicating and swineherding is typical of the sinners and Gentiles who were welcome to Luke's Church. Each of the main characters in the tale has an allegorical connection with the wider history of Jewish unresponsiveness and the readiness of sinners and Gentiles. It is not absolutely necessary to getting to the story's point but belongs in the richness of its full contextual meaning."

5. Jülicher, *Gleichnisreden Jesu*.

6. Brown, "Parable and Allegory," 36.

simple and direct, utilized to "illustrate the unfamiliar by the commonly familiar, to guide gently upwards from the easy to the difficult,"[7] in other words, from the everyday to the central message of the kingdom of God. Jülicher insisted that allegorical elements were absent from the unadulterated original parables of Jesus and that a parable can only have one point of comparison between the image and the reality which that image indicates. Modern scholars consider Jülicher's total rejection of any allegorical elements in Jesus' parables as a gross oversimplification, especially when properly considered within the rabbinic and OT contexts of the broader *mashal* genre. Others argue that certain Jesus parables can be rather complex and polyvalent, having more than one point of comparison and interpretation. Nonetheless, Jülicher's enduring contribution to parable exegesis is the insight that there exists a valid distinction between the parables of the historical Jesus and the parables as presented in the Synoptic Gospels.[8]

In this first chapter, I will summarize modern research on the parable of the Rich Man and Lazarus in Luke 16:19–31 as it has developed since Jülicher precipitated the end of the allegorical method's dominance at the close of the nineteenth century. Generally speaking, scholarly interpretation of the parable of the Rich Man and Lazarus has progressed in three different directions: the search for a parallel, the application of modern literary criticism, and the application of modern social-science criticism.

The first of these directions, the search for a parallel, is characterized by a vigorous search for parallel canonical and extra-canonical texts in an attempt to discover an appropriate literary and conceptual background against which to understand this perplexing parable. Scholars in this category range from those who assert direct literary dependence upon a specific proposed parallel text or collection of texts to those who claim no direct dependence upon any particular text or group of texts, but rather stress the resonances of common folkloric imagery and motifs across a variety of

---

7. Jülicher, *Gleichnisreden Jesu*, 1.146. Jülicher claimed that Jesus' parables were similes, not metaphors, and classified these under three forms: (1) a similitude (*Gleichnis*) in which there is a single point of comparison between an image (*Bild*) and the indicated reality (*Sache*) (1.58–80); (2) a parable (*Parabel*) which is a freely invented story that takes place in the past and challenges the hearer to form a judgment (1.92–111), and; (3) an example story (*Erzählung*) which is presented as an actual illustration of the reality it is meant to illustrate (1.112–15). As similes, Jülicher maintained that Jesus' parables were intended as direct speech that is simple, clear, and self-explanatory rather than metaphors that he considered as indirect speech that is enigmatic, means something other than what is stated, and so is vulnerable to allegorization.

8. Gowler, *Saying about the Parables*, 3–6.

canonical and extra-canonical writings from several cultural backgrounds upon which the parable appears to draw.

A second direction may be identified as the application of modern literary criticism to the interpretation of the parable. Scholars in this category interpret the parable with the tools of modern literary criticism, emphasizing the necessity of reading the parable from within its immediate literary and theological context, within the Lucan Travel Narrative, and within the Lucan Gospel as a whole. Others specifically examine how the parable functions to advance the Gospel's narrative and character development, how parable characters provide commentary upon characters in the wider Lucan narrative, and how the parable contributes to the Gospel's overall rhetorical thrust.

A third direction may be identified as the application of modern social-science approaches to the interpretation of the parable. Scholars in this category include those who concentrate on the social and cultural dynamics implicit within biblical texts in an effort to illuminate the parable's social and cultural world. The articulation of comprehensive social-science models of first-century Mediterranean society highlight pivotal dynamics not immediately evident to modern readers, such as limited-goods societies, honor-shame values, and patron-client relations.

Despite these developments, a dialogue between the literary and social-science methods with regard to the parable of the Rich Man and Lazarus is lacking. In his 1991 monograph entitled *Host, Guest, Enemy and Friend: Portraits of the Pharisees in Luke and Acts*, David B. Gowler proposes an interdisciplinary method that he calls the socio-narratological approach, an approach that integrates the insights from both literary and cultural analyses of biblical narratives. This approach is well-suited to a fresh understanding of the parable of the Rich Man and Lazarus from within its narrative and social contexts because it provides the crucial tools required to make explicit the often implicit dynamics of narrative character development and operative cultural scripts. Heretofore, there has been no comprehensive treatment of the parable of the Rich Man and Lazarus utilizing the interdisciplinary socio-narratological approach; such a comprehensive treatment will be the ultimate purpose and goal of this work. In this first chapter, however, I shall confine myself to summarizing modern research upon the parable according to the three general directions outlined above.

THE SEARCH FOR A PARALLEL

Gressmann's Proposal—An Egyptian Parallel

Although Jülicher was not directly concerned with the search for textual parallels, his commentary on Jesus' parables in general and on the parable of the Rich Man and Lazarus in particular inadvertently set off just such a vigorous search. Jülicher's assertion that a parable can only have one point of comparison between the image and the reality which that image indicates led him to understand that the Rich Man and Lazarus was composed of two originally distinct parts. According to Jülicher, the first part of the parable, vv. 19–25, was derived from Jesus and illustrates the eschatological reversal of the rich and poor men while the second part, vv. 26–31, was a secondary pre-Lucan addition that serves as an exhortation to repentance.[9] The depiction of the afterlife in the parable did not correspond to Jesus' own thinking, but rather reflected popular notions about postmortem existence that neither Jesus nor the evangelist felt compelled to modify or correct as these were not germane to the parable's central message.[10] This assertion, however, begged questions regarding the provenance of such popular notions about postmortem existence and what influence such notions might exercise over a proper interpretation of the parable.

Hugo Gressmann attempted to respond to the questions raised by Jülicher by proposing that the first part of the parable (vv. 19–26) is associated with Jesus and was based upon an ancient Egyptian folktale contained within a larger narrative of Setme Khamwas, the high priest of Ptah at Memphis and his divine son Si-Osire.[11] The folktale relates how Setme and Si-Osire observed the funerals of a wicked rich man buried with honor and a virtuous poor man buried without honor. Setme exclaims that he wishes to be treated as the rich man upon his death, to which Si-Osire objects and declares that the lot of the poor man is certainly more blessed. To prove the

---

9. Jülicher states that the evangelist adopted the parable in its present form with v. 26 serving as an editorial bridge uniting the two originally distinct parts (*Gleichnisreden Jesu*, 2.634, 638–39).

10. Ibid., 2.623.

11. Gressmann, *Vom reichen Mann*, 31–32. The folktale appears to have existed independently and was only secondarily attached to its present narrative context. The larger story narrates how Si-Osire, miraculously born to the childless couple Setme and his wife Mehuseke, was the reincarnation of the great magician Horus-son-of-Paneshe. At the age of twelve, Setme challenges and conquers a mighty Nubian sorcerer before returning to Amente.

point, Si-Osire takes his father on a tour of Amente, the realm of the dead, where he witnesses that in the afterlife the gods weigh good and evil deeds upon a scale of judgment. Whenever a person's evil deeds are greater, that person is punished; whenever a person's good deeds are greater, that person is taken to dwell among the gods. Thereafter, he sees the poor man now dressed in the rich man's fine linen clothing and seated in a place of honor near the god Osiris because his good deeds were more numerous than his evil deeds and yet he was not properly compensated during his earthly life. The rich man, on the other hand, was being punished since his evil deeds were more numerous than his good deeds and he was not properly punished during his earthly life.[12]

The only extant text of the folktale is a Demotic version from the second century C.E. written on the reverse of two unrelated business documents.[13] In Gressmann's estimation, the original version of the folktale circulated in ancient Memphis where it accrued some motifs about torture in Hades during the Hellenistic era. Jews living in Memphis and Alexandria became acquainted with the tale and orally transmitted it back to Palestine where it was retold and eventually appeared in several derivative rabbinic versions dating from the second to the fifth centuries.[14] Gressmann postulates that the similarities between the Lucan parable and these secondary rabbinic versions can be best explained by a common, though now lost, ancient Egyptian original.[15]

---

12. For an English translation of the folktale, see Lichtheim, *Ancient Egyptian Literature*, 3.138–51. See also Griffith, *High Priests of Memphis*, 42–43, and Maspero, *Popular Stories*, 144–53. Maspero ("Contes relatifs," 473–504) was the first to postulate a relationship between the Egyptian folktale and the Lucan parable, a fact which Gressmann acknowledged in *Vom reichen Mann*, 31–32.

13. One of the business documents dates from the seventh year of Claudius (46–47 C.E.). See Boring et al., *Hellenistic Commentary*, 227–28.

14. Gressmann (*Vom reichen Mann*, 70–86) presents these as texts A through G in the original Hebrew or Aramaic. The earliest of these versions is found in the Palestinian Talmud (*y. Sanh.* 6.6 23c, 30–41.42–43 and *y. Hag.* 2.2 77d, 42–54.54–57) about two Torah scholars and a tax collector Bar-Ma'yan. One scholar dies and is buried without the honor due his piety while the tax collector is buried with much honor. The other scholar is grieved over the apparent injustice but is consoled in a dream that funerals compensated for the singular good deed of the tax collector and the singular evil deed of the scholar. Thus compensated, in the afterlife the scholar is rightfully rewarded with otherworldly bliss in a garden containing a spring of water while the tax collector is rightfully punished by attempting in vain to reach the waters of a river with his tongue.

15. Gressmann, *Vom reichen Mann*, 53–54.

Finally, Gressmann asserts that Jesus was familiar with a version of the tale that he utilized in the first part of the Lucan parable (vv. 19–26) and that he provided it with a new conclusion that he intended as the real purpose of his teaching: to contradict the belief that it is possible to receive knowledge regarding the afterlife from otherworldly messengers (vv. 27–31).[16] Gressmann's proposal that the Demotic folktale is parallel to the Lucan parable appears at least superficially attractive primarily because of the juxtaposition of and contrast between rich and poor men in their earthly life and their ultimate reversal of fortunes in the afterlife. Moreover, it appears to supply an explicit and ethically satisfying criterion of judgment which is disturbingly absent in the Lucan parable.

Just a few years after Gressmann advanced his proposal for an Egyptian parallel, Rudolf Bultmann challenged its validity.[17] Bultmann asserted that the thrusts of the Egyptian tale and the Lucan parable were actually quite different. According to Bultmann, the Egyptian tale serves as proof of divine justice in that good and evil deeds are properly compensated in the afterlife with reward and punishment. The Lucan parable, on the contrary, demonstrates a balancing out of earthly fortunes in the afterlife without explicit reference to virtue or vice. Bultmann's treatment maintains Jülicher's bifurcation of the parable into two unequal parts, stating that vv. 19–26 portray an equalization of earthly destinies in the afterlife, intended as a consolation to the poor and a warning to the rich, and that vv. 27–31 demonstrate the futility of a miraculous return of a dead person to induce belief in God's will among the obdurate rich, made sufficiently evident in the books of Moses and the prophets.[18] He understands the latter point as a specifically Jewish message, one that he maintains could not originate with Jesus or the early church. Rather, Bultmann concludes with very great probability that the Lucan parable is a prime example of Jewish tradition being taken over by the early church and placed into Jesus' mouth in the synoptic tradition.[19]

Bultmann advances his own proposal that a Jewish legend about a rich and godless couple stands behind the Lucan parable. The legend relates how the curious wife opens a doorway leading to hell and is dragged inside. The husband lacks the courage to accompany a sympathetic giant to

---

16. Ibid., 56–59.
17. Bultmann, *Synoptischen Tradition*.
18. Ibid., 193, 212.
19. Ibid., 220.

attempt to rescue his wife and instead sends a servant boy. The boy finds the woman in terrible pain and thirst because of her multitude of sins, and in great despair because she does not have a son to pray for her release from suffering. The wife relays a message to her husband about the need to abandon evil and the great power of repentance, which her husband takes to heart and is eventually admitted into heaven.[20]

Bultmann's attempt to usurp Gressmann's proposal was unsuccessful. His counter-proposal for a parallel Jewish legend was not well received. Despite Bultmann's otherwise valid critique that the Egyptian folktale does not provide a convincing parallel to the Lucan parable, Gressmann's proposal maintained its credibility among scholars for nearly seven decades[21] until challenged with a more viable counterproposal by Ronald F. Hock.

Hock's Counterproposal—Greco-Roman Parallels

In a pivotal 1987 article, Hock bemoaned the decades-long absence of serious analysis that produced a stable, uniform, and almost self-satisfied scholarly tradition regarding the parable of the Rich Man and Lazarus. He tersely, yet accurately, summarized the ossified state of critical commentary as follows:

> Since Jülicher, scholars have virtually accepted as a given the division of the parable into two parts. Since Gressmann, scholars have looked to an Egyptian folktale for the background of at least the first part of the parable and for interpretation of details in the parable. And since Bultmann, scholars have increasingly had to decide whether Jesus or the church is the origin of the parts of the parable.[22]

Hock proceeded to critically evaluate and systematically dismantle this ossified scholarly tradition before constructing his own alternate proposal.

With regard to the proposed Egyptian folktale, Hock states that "the parallels between the two are neither as compelling nor as explanatory" as Gressmann suggests. Rather, only an indirect relationship may be claimed because a number of important differences exist, including that

---

20. For the text of the Jewish legend, see Lévi, "contes Juifs inédits," 65–83.

21. In fact, Jeremias (*Parables of Jesus*, 183) claims that the Egyptian folktale is essential for understanding the parable in detail and as a whole. Grobel ("Neves," 373–82) argues for the continued validity of Gressmann's proposal, albeit in modified form, based upon a speculative reconstruction attempting to explain the absence of the rich man's name in the Lucan parable.

22. Hock, "Lazarus and Micyllus," 451.

the contrasting funerals and the tour of the afterlife are both key elements in the folktale but play no role in the parable. Most importantly, according to Hock, the folktale does nothing "to clarify what is most opaque to interpreters of the parable, and that is the rationale for the reversal of fortunes of the rich man and Lazarus." The folktale's stated axiom—to the one who does good on earth, good is done in the afterlife and to the one who does evil on earth, evil—is too vague to elucidate the criterion of judgment for the parable. He accuses scholars of thereby inappropriately supplying their own criteria for the rich man's condemnation (his wealth, his neglect of Lazarus) and the poor man's exaltation (his poverty, his presumed piety, and dependence on God).[23] Hock concludes his critical evaluation of the foregoing scholarship, stating:

> In any case, the point here is that once again the folktale hardly proves "essential" for understanding the parable. In fact, if the folktale is not a close literary parallel, even for vv. 19–26, and if it does not clarify the parable where it is opaque, then I submit it is best after all these years to lay the Gressmann hypothesis to rest, certainly to question its assumed utility. Now also seems the right time to challenge Jülicher's division of the parable into two parts. For without the folktale to confirm this literary analysis, the division appears arbitrary. . . . [T]he notion of seeking two points also becomes unnecessary, as do the various complex tradition histories of the parable—that is, whether Jesus, Luke's tradition, or Luke himself is understood to have added a new conclusion to a familiar story of reversal.[24]

Thus liberated from the exegetical chains imposed by Jülicher, Gressmann, and Bultmann, Hock advances his own constructive alternate proposal regarding viable parallels. He argues that it is quite legitimate and indeed necessary to cast the comparative net wider to include literary texts from the contemporary Greco-Roman milieu, specifically rhetorical and Cynic texts that addressed the topic of wealth and poverty. Such rhetorical texts achieved their purposes by frequently providing a comparison (σύγκρισις) between extreme examples from contrasting groups, in this case the rich and the poor, along with further characterization (ἠθοποιία) achieved through dialogue. Hock cites the works of Lucian of Samosata

---

23. Ibid., 452–54.
24. Ibid., 454–55.

(d. 180), especially his *Cataplus* and *Gallus*,[25] as particularly illustrative for reconstructing the parable's social and intellectual milieu.

Both the *Cataplus* and the Lucan parable contain a comparison between extreme examples from contrasting groups. The nameless rich man in the parable and the rich tyrant Megapenthes in the *Cataplus* are extreme examples distinguished by their fine clothing and luxurious banquets, prominent indicators of their abundant wealth. Poor Lazarus in the parable and poor Micyllus in the *Cataplus*, on the contrary, suffer deprivation due to their lack of sufficient clothing and nourishment. Moreover, both rich men are further characterized by their consequent dialogues, protesting their reversed fortunes after death; the one bargains with the patriarch Abraham, the other with the fate Clotho. These dialogues reveal negative aspects of the rich men's interior attitudes and prior activity. Notably, both the parable and the *Cataplus* follow the same plot line, whereby the deaths of a rich man and a poor man are followed by their reversal of fortunes in Hades.

Hock reasons that the criterion of judgment, so opaque in the parable, becomes clearer when compared with that of the *Cataplus*: the divinity's wrath at the rich's use of wealth in the pursuit of hedonism—particularly the sexual immorality associated with banquets—that wealth facilitates and poverty inhibits. Far from a simply amoral description of wealth and poverty, the descriptions would evoke ethical connotations, and thus, a coherent criterion of judgment even if not expressly articulated in all instances:[26]

> Once the modern reader is aware that the ancient Greco-Roman milieu would include familiarity with comparisons made for contrastive purposes as well as with the harsh charges that were often made against the rich and especially against their hedonism, then the reversal of the rich man's fortunes and his lasting torment in Hades hardly comes as a surprise. His judgment is as obvious and as deserved as that of Megapenthes. And he deserved it, not merely because of what he failed to do, that is, feed Lazarus, but because of what he habitually did, that is, live hedonistically and immorally. Conversely, Lazarus is judged innocent and so finds lasting comfort in the bosom of Abraham, not so much because

---

25. For the text of the *Cataplus* and the *Gallus*, along with English translations, see Harmon, *Lucian*, 2.1–57; 2.171–239.

26. Hock, "Lazarus and Micyllus," 456–57, 461. Megapenthes, for instance, is judged for his numerous adulteries, incidences of ephebophilia, and violation of maidens, among other acts such as murder.

of his assumed faith as because his poverty, which excluded him from the damning life of the rich man.[27]

Richard J. Bauckham[28] generally agrees with Hock's assessment that the scholarly tradition's exclusive focus on the Egyptian folktale identified by Gressmann has had detrimental effects on the parable's interpretation. Such a focus has erroneously perpetuated the idea that the parable consists of two distinct parts rather than existing as a unified whole, and the equally erroneous assumption that the parable's criterion of judgment must therefore be similar to that of the Egyptian folktale.[29]

However, Bauckham criticizes Hock's counterproposal on the very same two counts that Hock criticized Gressmann. With regard to the parable's unity, he argues that the Lucian parallels do not clarify the parable's unity but seem to maintain the parable's division into two parts in the same way that the Egyptian folktale does, without reference to the motif of a dead person's return. With regard to the criterion of judgment, Bauckham states that Hock's transference of the criterion from the Lucian parallels to the Lucan parable is akin to the misguided transference of the criterion from the Egyptian folktale. This misuse of the parallel confuses the idea that the rich man of the parable is condemned not because of his self-indulgent feasts and associated sexual immorality, but because he lives in luxury while Lazarus lives in destitution without the implicit moralizing. This transference obfuscates the parable's stated criterion in v. 25 asserting that God's justice consists of an equal and opposite reversal of fortunes based upon one's social status and without reference to one's moral standing. The moral qualities of the two men are irrelevant.[30]

Bauckham states that Hock "is probably wrong to argue that [Lucian's *Cataplus* and *Gallus*] are *more* relevant to the interpretation of the parable than the Egyptian story is, but right to argue that they are *also* relevant."[31] One must not only recognize that parallels may utilize the same major narrative motifs, such as a postmortem reversal of fortunes or a dead person's return to the living, but how such parallels might utilize these narrative motifs differently from one another and from the parable. Bauckham concludes:

---

27. Ibid., 462.
28. Bauckham, "Rich Man and Lazarus," 225–46.
29. Ibid., 230.
30. Ibid., 232, 235–36.
31. Ibid., 234, (author's emphases).

It may be seen that the true significance of the parable emerges when attention is given to all available parallels, not restricted to one, and when attention is given to the parable's differences from, as well as its resemblances to the parallels. Comparison with the story of Setme and Si-Osiris, its Jewish derivatives, and Lucian's *Cataplus*, shows the parable's use of the theme of reversal of fortunes to be different from theirs in highlighting the injustice of gross material inequality as such. Comparison with the story of Si-Osiris, its Jewish derivatives, along with examples of the return of a dead person to reveal the fate of the dead to the living, shows that the parable's unity hinges on Abraham's unexpected refusal of the rich man's request, directing attention away from an apocalyptic revelation of the afterlife back to the inexcusable injustice of the coexistence of rich and poor.[32]

Bauckham's critique notwithstanding, Hock's counterproposal succeeded in overturning Gressmann's long-standing proposal and validated casting the figurative comparative net wider in the search for parallels to the Lucan parable. While Hock confined himself to literary texts from the contemporary Greco-Roman milieu, others expanded the search to include material from the Jewish apocalyptic tradition.

Nickelsburg—Resonances with Jewish Apocalyptic Texts

The questions that Jülicher elicited regarding the provenance of popular notions about postmortem existence and the influence such notions might exercise over a proper interpretation of the Lucan parable motivated Gressmann in 1918 to propose the Egyptian folktale as a parallel. Bultmann was not the only scholar to advance an alternate to Gressmann's proposal at an early date. Around that same time, L. W. Grensted in 1914 and A. O. Standen in 1921, apparently independently of each other, both noticed the similarities between the parable and parts of the book of *1 Enoch*. Grensted and Standen based their observations upon what they called "reminiscences" of the imagery and vocabulary contained in *1 Enoch* 22, principally the depiction of the separation of the righteous dead from the unrighteous dead in Hades, the former provided with light and a spring of water, the latter in darkness, deprived of water, and subjected to torments until the time of judgment.[33] The similarities do not extend much further, however, as the geography of Hades

---

32. Ibid., 236.
33. Grensted, "Enoch in St. Luke," 333–34, and Standen, "Dives and Lazarus," 523.

depicted in *1 Enoch* 22 with its western mountain of the dead containing four hollow places, three for the unrighteous dead and one for the righteous dead, does not correspond well with that of the Lucan parable.

More promising is the observation by Sverre Aalen in 1966 that a relationship of some sort exists between the last chapters of *1 Enoch* (i.e., *1 Enoch* 92–105, henceforth the Epistle of Enoch)[34] and the special L material in the Gospel of Luke, in which he identifies several "affinities" in vocabulary and expression. The affinities common to both the Epistle of Enoch and special L include the prominence of the subjects of justification and self-justification, the occurrence of some nearly identical and rare expressions, and the motif of sudden death as a result of God's judgment. These are bolstered by further correspondences in substance regarding views on the rich and the poor, on the mighty and the lowly, on punishment in Hades, and on a two-stage pattern of eschatology that allows for an intermediate state between death and the final consummation.[35]

This final point regarding the similarity in the pattern of eschatology is most pertinent for the parable of the Rich Man and Lazarus as it depicts the immediate separation of the righteous and sinners upon death, the former granted a period of rest and the latter subject to a period of preliminary punishment. The period of separation, presumably in Hades, does not preclude a future resurrection of both the righteous and sinners for a final great judgment and eternal disposition of their respective fates.[36] Consequently, this would seem to support the view that both the rich man and Lazarus are depicted in the parable as existing in an intermediate state in Hades before the advent of the final judgment, with the rich man suffering

---

34. According to Nickelsburg, *1 Enoch 1*, the book of *1 Enoch* is composed of five major divisions and two appendices: The Book of Watchers (chaps. 1–36), The Book of Parables (chaps. 37–71), The Book of Luminaries (chaps. 72–82), The Dream Visions (chaps. 83–90), and The Epistle of Enoch (chaps. 92–105, with chap. 91 as editorial). The Birth of Noah (chaps. 106–7) and Another Book of Enoch (chap. 108) are appendices.

35. Aalen, "Last Chapters of *I Enoch*," 1–6. Aalen also highlights similarities in concepts and expressions between the parables of the Rich Fool in Luke 12:15–21 and of the Rich Man and Lazarus in Luke 16:19–31 and those found in *1 Enoch*.

36. Such is the pattern of eschatology presented in the Book of Wisdom 1–5. The righteous dead are in an intermediate state of rest in the hand of God (4:7) and experience no torment (3:1). During their lives, they had experienced trials (3:5) and were objects of reproach by the wicked (5:3). The unrighteous dead, conversely, are in torment and pain (3:1; 4:19). During their lives they enjoyed good things (2:6) but trusted in their riches and were proud (5:8), were foolish (3:2; 5:4) and erred from the truth (5:6). They will appear in final judgment (3:13, 18). Cf. Aalen, "Last Chapters of *I Enoch*," 11–12.

preliminary punishments and Lazarus enjoying a preliminary period of rest in Abraham's bosom.[37]

The "resonances" identified by Grensted and Standen and the "affinities" isolated by Aalen are significant in that their contributions begin to move the scholarly discussion away from the search for purported parallel texts to the exploration for a commonality in literary imagery and motifs regarding attitudes toward wealth and poverty and notions of postmortem existence and retribution that more beneficially serve to elucidate a coherent literary and conceptual background against which to interpret the parable of the Rich Man and Lazarus.

George W. E. Nickelsburg explores at length Aalen's proposition that a relationship exists between the Epistle of Enoch and the special L material in the Gospel of Luke, especially with regard to what he calls a remarkably similar attitude toward the rich and their riches.[38] The Epistle of Enoch depicts a bitter conflict between the righteous and the sinners. The sinners are characterized in both religious terms—they are accused of idolatry and blasphemy—and in social terms—they are the rich and powerful who oppress, abuse, and persecute the righteous. The message of the Epistle is intended to strengthen and encourage the righteous that unjustly suffer violence and oppression at the hands of the sinners, and assure them that God will indeed adjudicate the blatant injustices of the present situation in the coming judgment.[39] This assurance is achieved by way of a series of apocalyptic visions:

> The author reveals, first of all, an imminent future in which the present injustices will be reversed, and the tensions which these have created will be alleviated. Moreover, he unfolds a revelation of an unseen heavenly realm that is *already operative* as the sphere of salvation. At this moment, the angels are operative as intercessors before the divine judge, and the names of the

---

37. Aalen, "Last Chapters of *I Enoch*," 8-10. Other correspondences include an analogous attitude toward the OT, to which the ungodly are held accountable for their rejection and perversion of the word of God and the covenant (compare 1 *Enoch* 99:2, 104:9, and Luke 16:31).

38. Nickelsburg, "Riches, the Rich, and God's Judgment," 324-44. In a subsequent article, Nickelsburg ("Revisiting the Rich and Poor," 579-605) states that both the author of the Epistle and the Lucan evangelist *"presume* a dualistic worldview that is based on revelation, although they embody their material in literary forms that are at home in sapiential literature rather than cloth [sic] it in apocalyptic visions," 579.

39. Nickelsburg, "Riches, the Rich, and God's Judgment," 327. Other Jewish apocalyptic texts, such as 4 Ezra and *Syriac Apocalypse of Baruch*, depict postmortem conditions and events that contribute to understanding the conceptual background of the parable.

righteous are inscribed in the register of the blessed, as a guarantee of the salvation to come.[40]

Furthermore, the author presents a chorus of exhortations addressed to comfort the suffering righteous while unleashing a litany of woes against the sinners for their mistreatment of the righteous, a sample of which from *1 Enoch* 96:4–8 will suffice to convey the caustic quality of the language and the explicit linkage between riches and the threat of judgment:

> Woe to you, sinners, for your riches make you appear to be righteous, but your heart convicts you of being sinners; and this word will be a testimony against you, a reminder of your evil deeds.
>
> Woe to you who devour the finest of the wheat, and drink wine from the krater, while you tread on the lowly with your might.
>
> Woe to you who drink water from every fountain; for quickly will you be repaid, and cease and dry up, because you have forsaken the fountain of life.
>
> Woe to you who commit iniquity and deceit and blasphemy; it will be a reminder against you for evil.
>
> Woe to you, mighty, who with might oppress the righteous one; for the day of your destruction will come. In those days, many good days will come for the righteous—in the day of your judgment.[41]

According to Nickelsburg, the Gospel of Luke, particularly the special L material, shares with the Epistle of Enoch the same basic attitude toward riches, namely, that "the accumulation and holding of riches and possessions are inversely related to the possibility of salvation."[42] Nonetheless, there are some subtle yet vital qualifications. The Epistle starkly views the rich and their possessions in a consistently negative light, asserting that the rich will inevitably be condemned in God's judgment and delivered over

---

40. Nickelsburg, "Apocalyptic Message," 325 (his emphasis). A good summary of the contents, structure, and message of the Epistle of Enoch is contained in this article. For a comprehensive and exegetical treatment of the epistle, see Nickelsburg, *1 Enoch 1*.

41. Nickelsburg, *1 Enoch 1*, 467.

42. Nickelsburg, "Riches, the Rich, and God's Judgment," 340. This assertion contradicts the Deuteronomistic axiom that contends that prosperity in one's lifetime proves that one is blessed by God and, by extension, that misery in one's lifetime proves that one is cursed by God.

to eternal punishment. The Gospel, on the other hand, nuances this view so that the rich and their possessions are not always depicted in a negative light, but rather only the rich who persist in the amassing and hoarding of wealth are subject to judgment and eternal punishment. The Gospel's attenuation of the Epistle's starkness allows for the real possibility of repentance among the rich, achieved through the active promotion of the sharing of possessions by way of almsgiving and deeds of generosity toward the poor, and even the radical alienation of personal wealth.[43]

Nickelsburg successfully demonstrates the potential utility of accessing the broader literary and conceptual background upon which the Gospel of Luke and particularly the parable of the Rich Man and Lazarus draws, referring to texts from the Jewish apocalyptic tradition like the Epistle of Enoch. Such Jewish texts illustrate attitudes toward the rich and beliefs regarding postmortem justice that are particularly beneficial when read alongside the parable. Arguably, this is a demonstrably more fruitful approach than the earlier search for purported literary parallel texts, as representatives of the current scholarly consensus such as Outi Lehtipuu and Klyne R. Snodgrass can agree.

Lehtipuu—Resonances with Contemporary Imagery and Motifs

Outi Lehtipuu[44] describes the scholarly movement away from attempts to identify fixed parallels and toward a more comprehensive understanding of the parable from within its literary and cultural context. The almost obsessive search for parallels to this particular parable in earlier scholarship can be characterized as a kind of "parallelomania,"[45] whereby there is a diligent search for similarities between two texts extracted from their proper contexts within larger narratives. Frequently, the similarities are exaggerated, the differences are minimized or glossed over, and conclusions drawn concerning the source, derivation, and significance of one or both

---

43. Ibid., 332, 340–41.

44. Lehtipuu, *Afterlife Imagery*. Lehtipuu's work is especially helpful for systematically tracing the development of afterlife imagery in Jewish and Greco-Roman texts, from the early undifferentiated common fate of the dead in Sheol and Hades to the later development of differentiated fates of rewards for the good and punishments for the evil.

45. See Sandmel, "Parallelomania," 1–13. Sandmel defines parallelomania as "that extravagance among scholars which first overdoes the supposed similarity in passages and then proceeds to describe source and derivation as if implying literary connection flowing in an inevitable or predetermined direction" (ibid., 1).

texts. Proceeding in this fashion involves a misuse of literary texts and is methodologically unsound. This is not to say that literary parallels do not exist or are not helpful, just that they need to be utilized more judiciously.

Rather than focusing strictly on purported parallels, Lehtipuu argues for the broader endeavor of intertextuality: "Instead of fixed parallels and direct dependency, we should speak of intertextual relations, common motifs and images that were used in the cultural milieu in the first century Mediterranean world."[46] In this regard, she posits that both contemporary Jewish and Greco-Roman accounts of the afterlife provide the nearest and most natural intertextual milieu for the parable of the Rich Man and Lazarus. Lehtipuu goes on to examine common and divergent depictions of postmortem existence in Jewish apocalyptic, Greco-Roman philosophical and other texts, and compares and contrast these with the depictions of the afterlife in the Gospel of Luke and in the parable. Her examination leads her to conclude:

> The reading of different sources shows clearly that the ideas on the afterlife took a similar form in the Hellenistic intertextual milieu. It is evident that different influences from Mesopotamia, Egypt, Persia, and Greece slipped into Judaism and evolving Christianity. Different ideas, motifs, metaphors, and images were freely borrowed; they were adopted, reused, and adjusted to earlier thinking. In new contexts, however, older ideas might have been used with different functions and for different purposes. That is why it is not possible to equate the use of a certain image in one story to that in another.[47]

On this basis, Lehtipuu contends that although the afterlife imagery in the parable may closely resemble many contemporary Jewish depictions, it cannot be taken *prima facie* that Luke's eschatological outlook consisted of an intermediate fate of some duration followed by a general resurrection. She argues that while the parable portrays the rich man and Lazarus in their individualized final states, elsewhere the Gospel presents a final, collective eschatological consummation of the end of time. This is an apparent contradiction that scholars should resist harmonizing into a coherent eschatological doctrine that Luke may or may not have possessed.[48]

---

46. Lehtipuu, *Afterlife Imagery*, 45.

47. Ibid., 302.

48. Ibid., 302–3. For Lehtipuu, eschatological expectations as presented in the Gospel were not central concerns, but rather were at the service of more practical issues such as exhortations to repentance and the right use of possessions.

Likewise, Klyne R. Snodgrass states that Jesus' parables should not be considered apart from their religious and cultural contexts, including appropriate reference to canonical and extra-canonical material. With specific relevance to the parable, Snodgrass refers to a wide range of texts from various contexts, including the OT (Deuteronomy, Isaiah, Ezekiel), the NT (James), early Jewish writings (Wisdom, *1 Enoch*, *4 Ezra*, *Testament of Judah*, *Psalms of Solomon*, Pseudo-Philo), Greco-Roman writings (Setme and Si-Osire, Plato, Plutarch, Lucian of Samosata), and later Jewish writings (talmudic and rabbinic texts).[49]

The question may legitimately be asked why modern scholars were so taken with the search for extra-biblical parallels in relation to the parable of the Rich Man and Lazarus. One reason may be the difficulty of reconciling the concept of eternal punishment with that of a merciful God, or else that the seemingly mechanical and impersonal nature of the reversal substituting one temporal inequality with an equal and opposite eternal inequality appears inconsistent with the notion of a loving, personal God. Another reason may be that if the afterlife imagery can be shown to be non-biblical in origin, then it and the socio-economic critique and ethical implications contained therein can also be ignored by society as somehow non-normative and non-binding.

Yet the search for a parallel to the parable of the Rich Man and Lazarus that occupied scholars through most of the twentieth century, while largely unsuccessful, cannot be called entirely unproductive. Gressmann's proposal for an Egyptian parallel drew attention to the validity of reading the parable over and against an extra-biblical text in order to gain insight into commonalities in narrative motifs such as the postmortem reversal of fortunes. Hock's counterproposal for the Greco-Roman parallels in Lucian of Samosata's *Cataplus* and *Gallus* highlighted the commonality of the rhetorical presentation of extreme contrasting examples and further characterization through dialogue. Nickelsburg's identification of resonances with Jewish apocalyptic in the Epistle of Enoch demonstrated the commonality of attitudes toward the rich and their possessions as well as further beliefs regarding postmortem imagery and justice. The current scholarly consensus summarized so concisely by Lehtipuu as the exploration of intertextual relations, common motifs, and images employed in the cultural milieu in the first-century Mediterranean world at once discounts and is indebted to the unsuccessful search for fixed parallels.

49. Snodgrass, *Stories with Intent*, 37–38.

MODERN LITERARY APPROACHES

A second direction that scholarly interpretation of the parable of the Rich Man and Lazarus has progressed since Jülicher is in the application of the tools of modern literary criticism, emphasizing the necessity of reading the parable from within its proper literary and theological context in Luke's Gospel. Additionally, others have examined how the parable functions to advance the Gospel's narrative and character development, how parable characters provide commentary upon characters in the wider Lucan narrative, and how the parable contributes to the Gospel's overall rhetorical thrust.

Literary and Theological Context in Luke's Gospel

Robert C. Tannehill[50] describes how Luke-Acts forms a narrative unity based upon the controlling concept of God's plan for universal human salvation and humanity's continual rejection of that plan. Jesus, as the central character in the Gospel, receives a divine mission to actualize God's plan of salvation (4:16–21). As the plot develops, Jesus encounters other characters that accept or reject his mission. On the one hand, the religious authorities, mainly the Pharisees and scribes, are generally portrayed as negative characters that reject God's purpose for themselves (7:30), and who are hypocritical (12:1), exalt themselves (14:11, 18:14), are self-righteous (16:15), and are lovers of money (16:14). These are the negative values from which the evangelist wants the reader to be disassociated. On the other hand, the disciples are generally portrayed as positive characters that leave all to follow Jesus (5:11, 28; 18:28), a detachment from possessions that is a key aspect of discipleship. They share in Jesus' authority over demons, and in the mission to cure disease and proclaim the kingdom (9:1–6), and recognize Jesus as Messiah (9:20). These are the positive values that the evangelist wants the reader to embrace. Nonetheless, they do struggle to understand how Jesus' suffering, rejection, and death fit into God's plan (9:45; 18:34) and fail in many other ways, including rivalry (9:46; 22:24)

---

50. Tannehill, *Narrative Unity*. Additionally, Talbert (*Literary Patterns*) demonstrates how the evangelist composed Luke-Acts according to a general pattern that included parallels between the career of Jesus in Luke and the career of the apostles in Acts. Both are baptized with the Holy Spirit, embark on ministries of preaching and healing, and conflict with religious authorities. Further parallels can be observed in the missionary journeys of Jesus and Paul. Such compositional technique, while aesthetically pleasing, more importantly serves to mutually interpret the significance of events in each work.

and apostasy (22:60–62). A third group, the crowds or the people, appear more differentiated in their response to Jesus. At first, great crowds from near and far respond positively by coming to hear Jesus teach and to be healed (6:17–19) and glorify God when they witness his mighty deeds (7:16–17). Later on, some in the crowds begin to respond negatively and even with hostility, an indication that an eschatological crisis is at hand that requires repentance and a definitive decision to either accept or reject Jesus (11:14–16, 23). "The story emerges as a dialogue between God and a recalcitrant humanity, rather than God's monologue."[51]

Internal narrative connections including the repetition and development of narrative motifs, type-scenes, and prophetic utterances further illustrate how Jesus goes about fulfilling God's plan of salvation. Such connections "provide internal commentary on the story, clarifying meanings and suggesting additional nuances" and contribute to the overall unity and coherence of the Gospel. For instance, the narrative motif of judgment-as-reversal appears in the Magnificat (1:46–55) as a demonstration of favor toward Mary that previews the favor toward the lowly and hungry and the disfavor toward the powerful and rich in the rest of the Gospel. Likewise, the Beatitudes and Woes (6:20–26) preview the blessing of the poor, hungry, and weeping and the cursing of the rich, satisfied, and laughing that is portrayed in various situations later on in the story. Another key narrative motif is that of the necessity of repentance, previewed in the preaching of John the Baptist. The Baptist warns that appealing to the patriarch Abraham for mercy cannot substitute for true repentance, described as the sharing of food and clothing with those in need (3:8, 10–11).[52]

According to Tannehill, the motifs of judgment-as-reversal and the necessity of repentance are echoed and developed in the parable of the Rich Man and Lazarus and provide a coherent literary and theological context within which to interpret it. The parable, while comforting to the poor, is primarily addressed as a warning to the wealthy to repent of their culpable negligence and assist the needy in their midst by demonstrating mercy as required by Moses and the prophets. In this connection, the implication is

---

51. Tannehill, *Narrative Unity*, 1.2. See also 1.1–2, 145–58 (the crowds), 167–72 (the religious authorities), and 201–6 (the disciples). God's plan for universal human salvation is only partially fulfilled by the end of Acts, highlighting the tension and rejection experienced by Jesus and the disciples that unifies the entire narrative work of Luke-Acts.

52. Ibid., 1.3, 28–29, 50–51, 206–10.

that the reader is to imitate the example of Jesus and the disciples rather than that of the religious leaders.[53]

John R. Donahue observes that the parables of Luke are in harmony with the major theological directions of the Gospel as a whole. Donahue highlights three of these theological directions that, incidentally, are prominent in the parable of the Rich Man and Lazarus. First, Luke shifts the locus of salvation from the end time to the present day, so that Christian eschatological existence means daily realization of the crisis brought to humanity by the life and teaching of Jesus. Second, conversion or repentance becomes a central theme in Lucan theology, the consequences of which affect all aspects of everyday life, including family, legal disputes, banquets, journeys, and the responsible use of wealth. Third, Luke emphasizes a theology of witness whereby faith must be demonstrated by action, a kind of Christian pragmatism that answers the question of "What shall I/we do?"[54]

Employing a more thematic approach, Luke T. Johnson[55] explores how the terms rich and poor function across the Luke-Acts narrative to refer to more than economic standing. Johnson asserts that these terms are used metaphorically to designate conditions of power and powerlessness, of human esteem or disdain, and most importantly, to symbolize human acceptance or rejection of the gospel message as proclaimed by the prophet Jesus:

> Luke takes with great seriousness both the literal problem and opportunity presented by men's actual use of and attitude towards possessions. He grasps the literal power possessions exert in centering and dominating men's lives. It is precisely this profound appreciation of the literal role of possessions that enables Luke to perceive the rich metaphoric possibilities to be found in the language of possessions for expressing the conditions of men's hearts.[56]

In this theological context, the parable of the Rich Man and Lazarus is directed by Jesus against the Pharisees who, on the one hand, claim to be keepers and defenders of the Law, but, on the other hand, are lovers of money and fail to observe the law of almsgiving. Johnson understands this context as indicating that "as the rich man had scorned the demands of the Law and the Prophets to give alms, so the Pharisees reject the teaching of

---

53. Tannehill, *Luke*, 251–54.

54. Donahue, *Gospel in Parable*, 204–11.

55. Johnson, *Literary Function of Possessions*. See also his further explorations in this field in *Sharing Possessions*.

56. Johnson, *Literary Function of Possessions*, 159.

the living Prophet Jesus on almsgiving," and ultimately that the rich man's rejection applies unmistakably to the rejection of those leaders and other rich who reject the person and message of Jesus.[57] Tannehill, Donahue, and Johnson, then, demonstrate the value and necessity of interpreting the parable with the Gospel's overall literary and theological context in mind.

Literary and Theological Context in the Lucan Travel Narrative

The Lucan Travel Narrative[58] forms a distinct and substantial literary unit within the Gospel, indeed comprising about one third of the total work. Frank J. Matera proposes that this journey narrative is composed of eleven discourses uttered by Jesus on his travel to Jerusalem, set off textually by changes in time and place. These discourses disclose a fundamental conflict between Jesus and Israel, exposing the contrasting points of view espoused by Jesus on the one hand and by the crowd and its religious leaders on the other:

> Jesus' discourses to the Pharisees and lawyers reveal conflicting points of view over ritual purity, the nature of the kingdom of God, Jesus' association with sinners, and the correct use of possessions. Whereas the Pharisees espouse an external purity, would exclude certain kinds of people from the kingdom, and are lovers of money, Jesus proclaims a purity that derives from almsgiving, sees an inherent contradiction in allegiance to possessions and allegiance to God, and views the appearance of the kingdom as a moment of great reversal.[59]

While some in the crowd are portrayed as favorably disposed toward Jesus and are potential disciples, most others are closer to the viewpoints of the religious leaders, failing to recognize the presence of the kingdom in Jesus' ministry and remaining unrepentant. For Matera, the parable of the Rich Man and Lazarus highlights the sharp contrast between Jesus who seeks God's esteem and views possessions as capable of alienating

---

57. Ibid., 143, 140–44.

58. There is disagreement regarding the extent of the Lucan Travel Narrative. The limits identified by Matera ("Jesus' Journey," 57–77) are those used in this work. Other scholars assert the Lucan Travel Narrative ends at 18:14 with the Synoptic Travel Narrative running from 18:15 through 19:27 (Fitzmyer, *According to Luke*); through 19:10 (Marshall, *Gospel of Luke*), and through 19:44 (Tannehill, *Luke*).

59. Matera, "Jesus' Journey," 74.

one from God and the Pharisees who seek human esteem, are lovers of money, and who fail to give alms.[60]

Kim Paffenroth[61] identifies a total of fourteen "L" parables, thirteen of which occur within the Lucan Travel Narrative and among which is numbered the parable of the Rich Man and Lazarus. These "L" parables are formally similar to one another on one or more of the following points: they contain dialogue and/or monologue, include one or more questions, possess contrasting or antithetical characters, can be considered example stories, and utilize reasoning from the lesser to the greater.[62] Additionally, Paffenroth observes that a certain similarity of content among "L" pericopae in general exists regarding narrative details. These narrative details, which Luke tends to omit in his redaction of Mark, involve the inclusion of numbers, personal and place names, and colorful details. Finally, the "L" pericopae evince a less radical and less negative attitude toward wealth and the wealthy and exhibit, among other topics, a concern for what it means to be a child of Abraham.[63] Most relevant for our study of the parable of the Rich Man and Lazarus is the discrepancy that Paffenroth highlights between the attitude toward wealth in the "L" material and the rest of Luke:

> The possession of wealth is depicted negatively in the L pericopae only when it has obscured or overridden the character's other

---

60. Ibid., 73–75.

61. Paffenroth, *According to L*. Paffenroth delimits his study to twenty-six pericopae in Luke 3–19 that he isolates as un-Lucan based on their dissimilarity to Lucan style and vocabulary in the rest of the Gospel, in an effort to reconstruct a hypothetical written pre-Lucan "L" source. He concludes: "The L material does seem to have enough dissimilarities from Lucan style, form and content to make it probable that this material is pre-Lucan. It also displays several internal consistencies of style, form and content, enough to make it seem unlikely that the material originated in a number of sources and traditions that accidentally overlapped in these unusual and un-Lucan ways" (ibid., 143).

62. Ibid., 97–98. The fourteen "L" parables identified by Paffenroth are: Luke 7:40–43; 10:30–37a; 11:5b–8; 12:16b–20; 13:6b–9; 14:28–32; 15:4–6; 15:8–9; 15:11–32; 16:1b–8a; 16:19–31; 17:7–10; 18:2–8a; 18:10–14a. Paffenroth observes that these are formally dissimilar from the parables Luke has taken over from Mark and Q in three ways: namely, that analogies are not drawn from nature or agriculture but from human interrelations, that none is explicitly a kingdom parable, and that there is a lack of allegorization.

63. Ibid., 117–38. See the three "child of Abraham" pericopae in Luke 13:10–17b, 16:19–31, and 19:2–10 in which a marginalized character suffers from some physical impairment, experiences a reversal that alleviates the impairment, and is reconstituted as a child of Abraham. Paffenroth identifies a total of nine thematic groupings among "L" pericopae: tax collectors, widows and lepers; love or compassion; hospitality; setting at night; prayer; watchfulness; children of Abraham; honor and shame, and; joy at finding the lost.

concerns, becoming the most important thing in his or her life. ... In all of the L pericopae, the proper attitude towards wealth is depicted as one of appreciation and generosity, but never renunciation. Given Luke's preference elsewhere in his double work for complete renunciation of wealth or possessions and his criticisms of the rich, the attitude found in L material seems distinguishable from Luke's own predilections.[64]

It is this attitude toward wealth and the wealthy that James A. Metzger[65] explores, albeit from a much different perspective. Metzger focuses his study on four parables in the Travel Narrative. Therein, Metzger notes a gradual yet uncompromising progression. Jesus first criticizes overconsumption by the wealthy. The wealthy landowner's unexpectedly bountiful harvest does not awaken generosity but the rapacious desire for further accumulation and overconsumption (12:16–21). The wealthy father of two sons welcomes back the wasteful prodigal with further feasting, to the anger of the elder son outraged by his father's condoning even further overconsumption (15:11–32). Jesus then mounts an outright critique of wealth itself. The dishonest steward who extracted exorbitant commissions from his master's debtors to fund a luxurious lifestyle is forced to cancel these commissions and hope for hospitality among those he defrauded (16:1–13). The rich man's postmortem reversal and Lazarus' exaltation serve as a climax and illustrates the stark criteria of judgment that condemns acquired and sustained personal wealth, regardless of whether one gives alms or not (16:19–31).[66] According to Metzger, Jesus as presented in the Travel Narrative asserts that the mere presence of personal wealth testifies to an unequal distribution of land and resources, and a more radical solution than almsgiving is required if the poor are to receive the good news announced in 4:16–19. The parable of the Rich Man and Lazarus, then, serves as the climax for Jesus' condemnation of wealth in the Travel Narrative:

> [It] codifies the breakdown of the redistributive systems of almsgiving and beneficence in meeting the very pressing needs of society's most vulnerable. . . . It fails in part because persons with access to excess too often elect to spend it on themselves. Moreover, both almsgiving and beneficence offer none of the lasting

---

64. Ibid., 123.
65. J. A. Metzger, *Consumption and Wealth*.
66. Ibid., 184–87.

structural changes that might truly be received as "good news" by the poor. Under such systems, the rich need not alter their consumption habits in the least and retain their wealth as well as all the power and privileges that come with it. The poor, meanwhile, though receiving occasional, temporary relief, remain poor and struggle to subsist.[67]

Metzger further asserts that Jesus' interactions with two rich men near the end of the Travel Narrative illustrate potential responses to Jesus' preaching. Jesus encounters the wealthy ruler in 18:18–23 who asks "Good teacher, what must I do to inherit eternal life?" (18:18), to which Jesus ultimately responds that he must sell all that he owns and distribute the money to the poor (18:22). Conversely, Jesus encounters the wealthy chief tax collector Zacchaeus in 19:1–10 who exclaims "Behold, half of my possessions, Lord, I shall give to the poor, and if I have extorted anything from anyone I shall repay it four times over" (19:8), to which Jesus proclaims that salvation has come to that house and that Zacchaeus is to be regarded as a son of Abraham (19:9). The overall effect is one that depicts Jesus in the Travel Narrative and conveying an uncompromising, sectarian position that if the wealthy wish to participate in God's kingdom, they must divest themselves of their wealth so as to no longer qualify as rich persons.[68]

What Matera, Paffenroth, and Metzger variously demonstrate is the extreme polarization that exists in the Lucan Travel Narrative between Jesus and his message of the mutual exclusivity between allegiance to possessions and allegiance to God and the social and religious elite that erroneously regards wealth and human esteem as indicators of divine favor.

Character Building and Rhetoric

John A. Darr[69] describes how Lucan characters are used rhetorically to persuade the reader to adopt a particular viewpoint and system of values (that of Jesus) and to reject another (that of the Pharisees). The evangelist achieves this effect by utilizing three major rhetorical strategies. First, authority is established in the Lucan narrative by the introduction of the narrator and God as utterly reliable and authoritative figures that provide

---

67. Ibid., 187.

68. Ibid., 187–88. This is a perspective that cannot be assigned to the Gospel as a whole.

69. Darr, *Character Building*.

trustworthy commentary on persons and events in the story. Second, a hierarchy of responses develops based upon the ability of various characters to see, hear, and respond appropriately to the divine will as manifested in the person, message, and activity of the protagonists. Finally, the juxtaposition of protagonists allows the reader to compare and contrast their significance and continuing influence.[70]

According to Darr, characters in Luke-Acts "are assessed on the basis of their interaction with the protagonists, especially Jesus. And the effect is reciprocal: protagonists are delineated and evaluated largely by the variety of responses they elicit from secondary and tertiary characters."[71] The cast of Lucan characters recognize and respond to Jesus and his message in a variety of ways, some more appropriately than others; however, the Pharisees are portrayed as an extreme example of how not to respond, and the reader is encouraged to repudiate their point of view and their system of values. The Pharisees are portrayed as spiritually obtuse and as prideful, money-loving, unjust, hypocritical, and unrepentant. Although they are exalted in their own minds and in the minds of others, they find disfavor in God's eyes. They oppose Jesus and by the end of the story they are clearly grouped with outsiders while sinners and the poor are regarded as insiders.[72]

John Paul Heil[73] asserts that all meal scenes in Luke-Acts, particularly Jesus' last Passover dinner with his disciples, anticipate in some fashion the fellowship to be enjoyed at the eschatological banquet in the kingdom of God. Heil identifies seven meal scenes that call for Jewish leaders to repent of their uncompassionate leadership and so share in the fellowship of repentant and forgiven sinners.[74] One of these seven meal scenes is the parable of the Rich Man and Lazarus that is used rhetorically to discourage readers from being like the money-loving Pharisees of the Lucan narrative:

> Instead of being lovers of money like the Pharisees, the audience is invited to repent *by relying upon God as the only one who can and will completely satisfy all their hungers* in the eschatological banquet, *by sharing the food they have to rectify social injustice* toward their

---

70. Ibid., 49–59.

71. Ibid., 41. Darr classifies characters in Luke-Acts into three groups: tertiary figures, like the crowds or the people; secondary figures, like the Pharisees and tax collectors, and; the protagonists, like Jesus, John the Baptist, and the apostles.

72. Ibid., 126.

73. Heil, *Meal Scenes*.

74. Ibid., 312. The seven meal scenes that call for Jewish leaders to repent are 5:27—6:5; 7:36–50; 11:37–54; 14:1–24; 15:1–32; 16:19–31, and; 19:1–10.

fellow human beings in need, and *by relating to the hungry poor so compassionately and hospitably as their fellow human beings* that they themselves have the courageous faith to become as the poor, the hungry, and the weeping, whom God will fully satisfy and make happy at the eschatological banquet in the kingdom of God.[75]

Lehtipuu[76] focuses her analysis on the characters presented in the parable itself and how Luke uses characterization to get readers emotionally involved and to persuade them to adopt his own ideology. She argues that since the Gospels are plot-centered, apsychological narratives, it is inappropriate to describe biblical characters with terminology such a "flat" and "round" from modern character-centered, psychological narratives. Rather, characterization in ancient literature is based upon stereotypes and group identity.[77]

This final point is a crucial insight. If the characters in the parable are stereotypical, though admittedly extreme, examples of members of the rich and the poor, then any positive or negative evaluation of them is relevant to other rich and poor characters presented in the wider Lucan narrative and vice versa. The criteria of judgment in the parable and in the wider narrative are likewise interrelated: "The moral evaluation of the characters [in the parable] must be concluded from the standards of judgment Luke has introduced previously in his story. 'Standards of judgment' refer to the values that are present in the narrative, either explicitly or implicitly, that give to the reader the basis to judge the goodness or badness of the characters and their actions."[78]

By depicting a reversal of the rich and the poor, then, the parable serves as a warning to the rich to repent and exhibit the correct use of wealth by concrete actions benefiting the poor:

> The characterization of the rich man and the poor man Lazarus also serves this purpose. Both characters are stereotypes of their representative groups; one with wealth, the other without it. The detailed description of them, with purple and linen, bleeding sores and licking dogs, creates an illusion of reality around them. As the characters are presented vividly, the reader is guided to get emotionally involved in their story. Showing what happens to these

---

75. Ibid., 309, (author's emphases). See also Heil's exposition of the parable, *Meal Scenes*, 131–45.

76. Lehtipuu, "Characterization and Persuasion," 73–105.

77. Ibid., 73–81.

78. Ibid., 94. Such standards of judgment about wealth and poverty are given in John the Baptist's preaching in 3:7–14 and in Jesus' teaching in 6:20–26.

lifelike characters is a powerful rhetorical device. Its purpose is to lead the reader to [the] right kind of action and to share Luke's ideological view. In this way the point of the parable is very similar to the overall point of Luke-Acts.[79]

Modern literary approaches to the parable have made several significant contributions to a better understanding of the Rich Man and Lazarus. Tannehill's description of Luke-Acts as a narrative unity places the parable within the greater controlling concept of God's plan for universal human salvation and humanity's continual rejection of God's plan. The parable illustrates in dramatic fashion the ultimate consequences for acceptance or rejection of the divine plan, and hence the necessity of repentance among the rich. Metzger's reading of the Travel Narrative presents an even more radical reading of the parable, one through which Jesus conveys an uncompromising, sectarian position that if the wealthy wish to participate in God's kingdom they must divest themselves of wealth so as to become poor. Finally, Lehtipuu demonstrated that since Luke's characterization of the rich and the poor are stereotypical representations of their respective groups, then any positive or negative evaluation of them is relevant to other rich and poor characters presented in the wider Lucan narrative as well as in the parable. The rhetorical effect of such characterization is to persuade the reader to share Luke's ideological point of view and system of values.

MODERN SOCIAL APPROACHES

A third direction that scholarly interpretation of the parable of the Rich Man and Lazarus has progressed since Jülicher is in the application of modern social-science approaches that concentrate on the social and cultural dynamics implicit within biblical texts in an effort to illuminate the parable's social and cultural world. Most valuable in this endeavor is the articulation of comprehensive social-science models of first-century Mediterranean society that highlight pivotal dynamics not immediately evident to modern readers, such as limited-goods societies, honor-shame values, and patron-client relations.

---

79. Ibid., 104.

Cultural Studies

Kenneth E. Bailey[80] explores Gospel texts as they might be understood from an ancient Middle Eastern cultural perspective. Bailey's reading of the parable of the Rich Man and Lazarus illustrates several cultural indicators to which modern Western readers might otherwise be oblivious, especially as these pertain to the portrayal of the rich man's behavior and speech. With such cultural awareness, the rich man emerges as a decidedly repulsive character that is elitist, godless, and shamelessly manipulative of family ties. The rich man's elitist mentality is evident in the conspicuous consumption by which he not only indulged his own extravagant desires but publicly advertised such for his neighbors' adulation. The impression is reinforced in the postmortem dialogue with Abraham whereby he demands services of Lazarus, a person of the non-elite class whom he despises and refuses to address directly. The rich man cannot imagine a reality that is not socially and economically stratified, a reality in which he enjoys pride-of-place even in the afterlife. He is also godless given that he publicly feasted even on the Sabbath, preventing himself, his guests, and his servants from observing the day of rest and hearing the Law and the Prophets read in the synagogue. If he were observant and God-fearing, he would have heard that the Scriptures demand compassion for the poor and would have acted accordingly.[81]

Finally, the rich man is shameless, impudent, and argumentative in his dialogue with Abraham. Appealing for the mercy he knows the patriarch is honor-bound to acknowledge, he instead insults Abraham's honored guest, and by extension Abraham himself, with his request for Lazarus to fetch water to quench his thirst. His appeal is also a thinly veiled hint that he would like to join Abraham at the banquet. Rather than submit to Abraham's order to remember, the rich man shamelessly disobeys and posits a second request that Lazarus warn his brothers. Abraham's terse reply is that they should hear and obey the Law and the Prophets. Unaccustomed to having his orders rebuffed, the rich man goes so far as to attempt to contradict and correct the patriarch Abraham as he would a lowly inferior. Such impudence is intolerable, but Abraham replies with the finality that

---

80. Bailey, *Middle Eastern Eyes*.

81. Ibid., 382–87. Bailey makes much of the dogs in the parable, stating that they are most likely the rich man's vicious guard dogs that nonetheless demonstrate friendship and compassion toward Lazarus by doing what they can to heal the festering wounds while the rich man did nothing. These unclean animals are better than the rich man or, conversely, the rich man is worse than a dog.

such people will not repent even if someone rises from the dead.[82] Bailey concludes by alluding to Jesus' proverb on the impossibility of serving God and mammon in Luke 16:13:

> The parable reflects the corrupting, blinding *potential* of wealth and is critical of the socially irresponsible wealthy. The rich man used his resources for his own self-indulgent living. He cared nothing about his God, his staff or the needy in his community. Even in hell he remained unrepentant and continued to see Lazarus as an inferior who should serve him as a waiter or an errand boy. Mammon had become his master.[83]

Economic and Social Conflict

Halvor Moxnes[84] examines the social and economic systems as portrayed in the Lucan narrative world, with particular attention to the negative depiction of the Pharisees as lovers of money (16:14). Moxnes does so from the perspective of what he calls the moral economy of the peasant, a perspective of the underprivileged and disenfranchised poor who dwell at a subsistence-level existence. In a worldview wherein all material and immaterial goods exist in limited and fixed quantities, and any increase in goods possessed by one necessitates the decrease in goods possessed by another,[85] the Lucan Pharisees emerge as representatives of the elite rich.

From the Lucan perspective, wealth is not morally disreputable in and of itself, although it could be and frequently was obtained in morally disreputable ways. More importantly, the disposition of wealth has moral implications. Morally good uses of wealth are depicted in the parables of Luke 15 wherein the protagonist rejoices with others at finding the lost sheep, the lost coin, and at the return of the prodigal son. The implication is that someone who had experienced good fortune was obliged by honor to share this celebration with others in the village, a celebration that naturally would include the sharing of a meal or feast. Similarly, the parable of the Great Banquet in Luke 14 demonstrates how a feast originally intended for the elite rich is redirected to the non-elite and destitute poor. A morally

---

82. Ibid., 388–94.
83. Ibid., 395 (author's emphasis).
84. Moxnes, *Economy of the Kingdom*.
85. Ibid., 76–79. Malina, *New Testament World*, 90–116 more fully describes the limited-goods worldview.

evil use of wealth is depicted in Luke 12 in the parable of the Rich Fool, who rather than share his good fortune at an abundant harvest chose to avariciously guard that wealth and rejoice only with himself. Similarly, in Luke 16 the rich man neglects to share his wealth with the needy in the community, poignantly represented by Lazarus:

> The beggar Lazarus lies outside his gate while the rich man carries on his feast inside, probably with friends of his own status and group. The stereotypical expression of "rejoicing/feasting," together with the description of the rich man's luxurious clothes, puts this man into the category of the selfish, arrogant rich who do not share with others, who keep aloof from common and needy people. Thus, the description of the rich man clearly indicates a moral judgment; with his description of the exterior, Luke has indicated the character of this person.[86]

According to Moxnes, then, Luke condemns the conspicuous consumption as practiced by the elite rich, and by extension the Pharisees, as creating and maintaining distinctions that effectively exclude others. Rather than practicing almsgiving and other redistributive mechanisms that represent morally good uses of wealth, the rich accumulate and protect surplus wealth and thus prevent the poor from fulfilling even the most basic needs for food, clothing, and shelter, and in the extreme case of Lazarus, life.

> Underlying the criticism of the "merrymaking" of the rich was the assumption that wealth acquired by the rich was never shared with the common folk of the village, but circulated only among themselves. Thus, the inequality that existed in the first place was emphasized by the way in which the rich spent their wealth; not for the common good, but to protect their own position as a group over and against the needy people of the village.[87]

Within the context of a limited-goods worldview, Luke's argument is for an economy of the kingdom based on need and directed toward production for use rather than geared toward accumulation and preservation. The Lucan Jesus is presented as condemning the self-serving banquets of the elite rich with their exclusive guest list of friends, brothers, kin, and rich neighbors and instead asserting an alternative vision of disinterested banquets to which the stereotypically poor, maimed, lame, and blind were invited

---

86. Moxnes, *Economy of the Kingdom*, 89.
87. Ibid., 88–89.

as guests (14:12–14).[88] The former implied the expectation of a return, the latter precluded that possibility.

In a similar though decidedly more polemic approach, William R. Herzog[89] argues that Jesus' parables depict how oppression of the poor served the interests of the rich elite, and how human beings could respond to break the spiral of violence and cycle of poverty created by exploitation and oppression. Parables functioned as codifications that exposed political and economic exploitation of the poor by the rich and that demystified the forms of legitimization used to sanctify such oppression.[90] According to Herzog, the parable of the Rich Man and Lazarus represents the conflict between two social classes—the urban elites who had nearly everything and the desperate expendables who had almost nothing:

> Such wealth could be obtained only by the systematic exploitation of the poor, and it could be maintained only by their continual oppression. The urban elites who lived at the expense of the poor twisted Torah and Temple to serve their ends. They read the Prophets for their comfort and Moses to study the purities lest they should become unclean. Their wealth and its use in conspicuous consumption, their rapacious greed and its extraction of any surplus from the poor, their pursuit of power and privilege with its accompanying suppression of the people of the land, all these characteristics of the rich man's class reveal that its wealth is no sign of blessing but a curse on the land.[91]

According to Herzog, the Lucan Jesus' parable presents the subversion of the established order by removing the sacred legitimization utilized to perpetuate the *status quo* of oppression and exploitation. The popular expectation is that the rich man, surrounded by signs of God's blessings in life, would rest in Abraham's bosom after death and that Lazarus, apparently cursed in life, would be relegated to flames. Jesus, the pedagogue of the oppressed masses, exposes the lie:

> The reversal of the expected fates undermined not simply the hearers' view of the afterlife but, more importantly, their assumption

---

88. Ibid., 129.

89. Herzog, *Subversive Speech*.

90. Ibid., 3, 27. Herzog notes how his interpretations are inspired by the liberation-theological analysis and praxis of Paulo Freire as an aid to understanding the liberation-theological analysis and praxis of Jesus.

91. Ibid., 128.

that present circumstances could be used as a reliable guide for discerning God's judgments, or, to put the matter more pointedly, that social class was an indicator of divine blessing or honorable status. Once this connection had been broken, the assorted rural poor of Galilee or Judea who heard the parable could inquire into reasons for their misery that were much closer to home.[92]

Social-Science Models

The formal application of the tools of cultural anthropology and other social sciences to the exegesis of biblical texts, intended to complement traditional historical-critical methods, emerged in the 1980s with the articulation of comprehensive models of first-century Mediterranean society. Social-science models make explicit the social values, cultural dynamics, and worldview implicit in biblical texts to which modern readers might otherwise remain oblivious. Models attempt to provide a contextual framework for better understanding the social and cultural worldview of the text from within a first-century Mediterranean consciousness. Many models exist, but only two will be summarized here as being especially relevant to the parable of the Rich Man and Lazarus.

Bruce J. Malina[93] describes honor and shame as pivotal values of the first-century Mediterranean worldview. According to Malina, honor is a person's own claim to worth plus the public acknowledgement of that worth. Without social acknowledgement, one's claim of worth lacks merit and deserves ridicule. One's honor can be ascribed, that is, associated with the status of one's birth; or it can be acquired, achieved through positive social actions such as public acts of generosity or heroism. Honor, like all other goods, is a limited commodity and therefore must be jealously guarded against loss. Nearly every social interaction outside the family unit is a potential threat to one's honor. In this agonistic cultural context, words and deeds take on heightened significance especially among social equals where public interactions become challenge-riposte contests for maintaining, gaining, or losing honor. Shame is a positive value whereby a person has the proper sensitivity to act in accord with one's honor status; those who fail in this regard are shameless. One's honor status entails three areas: power (the hierarchical ability to control others), gender (adherence to defined male/

---

92. Ibid., 129.
93. Malina, *New Testament World*.

female roles), and religion (adherence to appropriate relationships within a fixed hierarchy of superiors and subordinates).[94]

Honor-shame values are operative in a variety of ways in the parable of the Rich Man and Lazarus and aid in its interpretation. For instance, the rich man comes across as utterly shameless for failing to adhere to his appropriate hierarchical relationship as a subordinate by daring to become argumentative with the patriarch Abraham. Additionally, given that honor is a limited commodity, the rich man correctly perceives that Lazarus' dramatic postmortem increase in honor status is detrimental to his own honor, now dramatically and publicly decreased.

Halvor Moxnes[95] defines patronage in the following way:

> Patron-client relations are social relationships between individuals based on a strong element of inequality and difference in power. The basic structure of the relationship is an exchange of different and very unequal resources. A patron has social, economic, and political resources that are needed by the client. In return, a client can give expressions of loyalty and honor that are useful to the patron.[96]

While inherently unequal, the patron-client relationship is mutually beneficial on several counts. Patrons have instrumental, economic, and political resources and can offer clients support and protection. Clients, in turn, can offer non-tangible resources such as solidarity and loyalty and provide an outlet for public expressions of generosity that enhance the patron's honor. When the social distance between patron and client is too great, a broker serves as an intermediary figure to bridge the gap.

Luke's Gospel presumes the existence of the patronage system but is critical of the behavior and attitudes of rich patrons and religious leaders on two counts: they accumulate wealth for themselves while denying just redistribution to their poor clients and they inhibit rather than facilitate access to the Holy. The Pharisees are portrayed as members of the rich elite who fail both as patrons who accumulate rather than redistribute wealth to needy clients and who fail as brokers who inhibit rather than facilitate access to God. The conflict between Jesus and the Pharisees can be understood in this context as a struggle for who is a more authentic broker

---

94. Ibid., 28–62. These honor-shame values are applicable on a collective as well an individual basis. See also Malina and Neyrey, "Honor and Shame," 25–65.

95. Moxnes, "Patron-Client Relations," 241–68.

96. Ibid., 242.

between God and the people.[97] Likewise, the rich man in the parable is shown to fail grievously in that he refused to recognize poor Lazarus as an actual or potential client in desperate need of his assistance and protection.

Modern social approaches have made significant contributions to better understanding the parable of the Rich Man and Lazarus from within its appropriate social and cultural context. Bailey explores Gospel texts as they might be understood from an ancient Middle Eastern cultural perspective. His reading of the parable with attention to the cultural indicators of the rich man's behavior and speech reveals a character that is decidedly repulsive, one that is elitist, godless, and shamelessly manipulative of family ties. Moxnes demonstrates how Luke condemns conspicuous consumption as practiced by the elite rich, and by extension the Pharisees, as creating and maintaining distinctions that effectively exclude others. Rather than practicing almsgiving and other redistributive mechanisms that represent morally good uses of wealth, the rich accumulate and protect surplus wealth and thus prevent the poor from fulfilling even their most basic needs for food, clothing, and shelter. Finally, Malina's exposition on honor and shame as pivotal values of the first-century Mediterranean worldview allows the reader to appreciate that since honor is a limited commodity, Lazarus' postmortem increase in honor necessitates the rich man's decrease in honor. The rich man is revealed as utterly shameless in his argument with the patriarch Abraham.

SOCIO-NARRATOLOGICAL APPROACH

Despite the foregoing modern developments summarized above, a dialogue between the literary and social-science methods with regard to the parable of the Rich Man and Lazarus is still lacking. David B. Gowler proposes an interdisciplinary method that he calls the socio-narratological approach, an approach that integrates the insights from both literary and cultural analyses of biblical narratives.[98] While Gowler's monograph concentrates on the overall characterization of the Pharisees in Luke-Acts, this approach is well suited to a fresh understanding of the parable of the Rich Man and Lazarus from within its narrative and social contexts because it provides the crucial tools required to make explicit the often implicit dynamics of narrative character development and operative cultural scripts—culturally conditioned patterns of perceiving and behaving.

97. Ibid., 254–57.
98. Gowler, *Host, Guest, Enemy and Friend.*

Modern Research on the Parable of the Rich Man and Lazarus (Luke 16:19–31)

The socio-narratological method is essentially a two-step process. First, the method begins with an evaluation of characters that populate a particular biblical text based upon scales of descending reliability and explicitness. Most explicit are direct definitions that vary on a scale of reliability from high to low. Direct definitions with high reliability are those with absolute authority: (a) the omniscient, reliable narrator; (b) Jesus, and; (c) the voice from heaven. Other characters may also serve as highly reliable witnesses when presented as under the inspiration of the Holy Spirit. Still other characters have varying degrees of reliability, least of all Jesus' opponents. Less explicit are indirect presentations that display the qualities and traits of characters, but leave it up to the reader to make appropriate inferences, thus resulting in varying degrees of authority, reliability, and explicitness. Indirect presentation is the primary means of characterization in Luke-Acts and takes the forms of speech, action, external appearance, environment, and comparison/contrast. Even where direct definitions do occur, they are frequently supplemented and corroborated with indirect presentations.[99]

The method's second step is the observation of the cultural norms that reflect upon the characters and their presentation in the text. It is at this point that the relevant cultural scripts are highlighted and integrated into the process of apprehending the narrative development of the characters in question. The social-science models of first-century Mediterranean society are indispensable in this regard, as they help illuminate operative values, social dynamics, and worldview such as honor-shame values, patron-client relations, perception of limited goods, purity-pollution boundaries, and kinship relations.[100] Gowler summarizes the goal of the socio-narratological approach in the following way:

> A socio-narratological approach seeks to integrate these two concerns [narrative analysis and cultural scripts] into a cohesive methodology, where a narrative-critical perspective of characterization is merged with a knowledge of the socio-cultural and literary patterns of communication in the first century and inherent in the text of Luke-Acts. In effect, not only *can* cultural contexts be merged with character analysis, but, in order for character analysis to be done correctly, cultural scripts *must* be utilized.[101]

---

99. Ibid., 181–82. See further Gowler, "Characterization in Luke," 54–62.
100. Gowler, *Host, Guest, Enemy and Friend*, 15–26.
101. Ibid., 27 (author's emphases).

Heretofore, there has been no comprehensive and exclusive treatment of the parable of the Rich Man and Lazarus utilizing the interdisciplinary socio-narratological approach; such a comprehensive and exclusive treatment will be the ultimate purpose and goal of this work. At this juncture, however, chapter 2 will be dedicated to highlighting some key dynamics operative in a subset of Lucan Travel Narrative parables, along with establishing a fresh translation of the text of the parable of the Rich Man and Lazarus, decisions on variant readings, and proposals for the parable's structure, unity, and authenticity. It will also consider the parable's placement and function within the context of the Lucan Travel Narrative and within the context of the Lucan Gospel as a whole.

2

The Parable of the Rich Man and Lazarus and the Lucan Travel Narrative Parables for the Repentance of the Rich

IN CHAPTER 1, I summarized modern research on the parable of the Rich Man and Lazarus in Luke 16:19–31 as it has developed since Jülicher. As we have seen, scholarly interpretation of this parable has progressed in three different directions: the search for a parallel, the application of modern literary criticism, and the application of modern social-science criticism. After this review of modern research on the parable of the Rich Man and Lazarus, it is necessary in this chapter to take a preliminary look at the parable from within its context in the Lucan Gospel and particularly from within its situation in the Lucan Travel Narrative, only thereafter proceeding with a detailed socio-narratological analysis in chapters 3 and 4. How does the parable of the Rich Man and Lazarus cohere with the rest of the Gospel and with the Travel Narrative on the issue of wealth and on the necessity of repentance among the rich? How does the parable argue its case and achieve the effect of persuading the rich to repent? What logical structures and strategies—parabolic dynamics—are employed within the parable to move the reader from a vision of reality that is exclusive and elitist to a vision that is inclusive, egalitarian, and associated with Jesus' preaching of the kingdom of God?

Tormented in Hades

The objective of this second chapter, then, is threefold: first, to isolate a subset of seven parables from the Lucan Travel Narrative that evince a certain affinity with regard to persuading the rich to repentance; second, to examine four shared parabolic dynamics by which these parables achieve their purpose; and third, to present the text of the parable of the Rich Man and Lazarus, its structure, and some brief preliminary exegetical notes that illustrate how these parabolic dynamics operate within this specific parable. Thus, this second chapter will properly situate the parable of the Rich Man and Lazarus as one of seven Lucan Travel Narrative parables that together argue for the necessity of repentance among the rich.

LUCAN TRAVEL NARRATIVE PARABLES FOR THE REPENTANCE OF THE RICH

A subset of seven parables may be distinguished in the Lucan Travel Narrative as possessing certain affinities in terms of their rhetorical strategy for persuading the rich to repentance. This subset consists of the following narrative parables: the parable of the Good Samaritan (10:30–35); the parable of the Rich Fool (12:16–20); the parable of the Great Banquet (14:16–24); the parable of the Prodigal Son (15:11–32); the parable of the Dishonest Steward (16:1–8); the parable of the Rich Man and Lazarus (16:19–31); and the parable of the Pharisee and the Tax Collector (18:10–14). For the sake of convenience, and taking a cue from 16:14, I will hereafter call this subset of seven parables φιλάργυροι parables because they are addressed to the money-loving rich characters of the Gospel whom Jesus challenges to repentance.

Each of these seven φιλάργυροι parables exhibit all or most of the following affinities that characterize this subset: They (a) are addressed by Jesus to one or more rich characters in the Gospel narrative; (b) demonstrate the need for repentance in the form of almsgiving or other merciful practices; (c) provide graphic and sometimes extreme characterizations of rich and/or poor characters; (d) utilize a rhetorical structure of reversal that involves orientation, disorientation, and reorientation, and; (e) are special "L" parables[1] that exhibit a less radical and less negative attitude toward wealth and the

---

1. Paffenroth (*According to L*, 97–98, 143) isolates twenty-six pericopae in Luke 3–19 that he attributes to a pre-Lucan "L" source based on their dissimilarity to Lucan style and vocabulary in the rest of the Gospel. Among these pericopae are fourteen special "L" parables: Luke 7:40–43; 10:30–37a; 11:5b–8; 12:16–20; 13:6b–9; 14:28–32; 15:4–6; 15:8–9; 15:11–32; 16:1b–8a; 16:19–31; 17:7–10; 18:2–8a; 18:10–14a.

wealthy when compared with other material in the Gospel. A short survey of each of these seven φιλάργυροι parables in terms of these affinities will demonstrate their coherence as a subset within the Lucan Travel Narrative.

At the outset of this chapter, it is important to keep in mind that for Luke the terms "rich" and "poor" do not refer exclusively to the sphere of economic existence. Rather, as Luke T. Johnson points out, they are employed as literary and metaphorical terms that refer to classifications of characters and their response or lack of response to God in the person of Jesus and to humanity:

> The use of the terms rich and poor in Luke's Gospel go beyond the designation of economic circumstances to express conditions of powerlessness and power, being outcast by [people] or accepted by [them]. The preaching of the Gospel to the poor and the proclamation of woes to the rich signify that by God's visitation in the Prophet Jesus, these conditions are reversed, that the outcast are called to salvation and the [ones] who enjoy present acceptance are to be rejected. In the working out of the narrative, the poor are to be found in those who respond to the prophet, particularly the sinners and tax-collectors. . . . [T]he rich are found in those who reject the prophet, the leaders and particularly the Pharisees and Scribes.[2]

The Good Samaritan (10:30–35)

Jesus addresses the parable of the Good Samaritan to a lawyer (νομικός) who stood up to test him with regard to the fulfillment of the Law and the inheritance of eternal life (10:25), followed up with a question intended to delimit who is to be considered a neighbor (10:29). The lawyer, as a representative of the religious elite and of the rich, is exhorted by Jesus at the conclusion of the parable to go and likewise show mercy (10:36–37). Elsewhere in the Gospel, lawyers are grouped together with the Pharisees as those who reject God's purpose for themselves by not being baptized by John (7:30), a baptism that implied bearing fruits that befit repentance (3:8). The narrative frame of the parable makes it clear that it is addressed to the rich and urges their repentance in the form of demonstrating mercy beyond the traditionally restricted understanding of neighbor as fellow Israelite.[3] Incidentally, the conjunction

---

2. Johnson, *Literary Function of Possessions*, 165–66.

3. See Lev 19:18: "Take no revenge and cherish no grudge against your own people. You shall love your neighbor as yourself. I am the LORD."

of the themes of the Law, eternal life, and the delimitation of neighbor resonates well with the parable of the Rich Man and Lazarus.

Within the parable itself, two rich characters, the priest and the Levite, are starkly characterized by their lack of compassion for the victim on the road to Jericho. The victim is passive yet graphically described as stripped, beaten, and half-dead. The Samaritan, in contrast, is characterized by his compassionate actions toward the victim, which are related in detail: "But a Samaritan traveler who came upon him was moved with compassion (ἐσπλαγχνίσθη) at the sight. He approached the victim, poured oil and wine over his wounds and bandaged them. Then he lifted him up on his own animal, took him to an inn and cared for him" (10:33–34). The verbal instructions to the innkeeper serve to reveal the Samaritan's true character as one who, although rich, practices genuine compassion toward the poor. The structure of the parable disorients and reverses the reader's expectations of who properly fulfills the Law, not the priest, not the Levite, but the Samaritan.

As one of the fourteen special "L" parables, the parable of the Good Samaritan is less radical in its attitude toward wealth and less negative toward the wealthy than the rest of Luke's Gospel. Here, as in the other φιλάργυροι parables, the parable does not advocate the complete renunciation of wealth and possessions but rather the proper use of such for almsgiving as compassionate care of victims. Likewise, the negative portrayal of the rich priest and rich Levite as representatives of the privileged social and religious class is balanced by the positive portrayal of the rich Samaritan held up as an example to be imitated.

The Rich Fool (12:16–20)

Jesus addresses the parable of the Rich Fool to the crowd in response to an individual requesting Jesus' arbitration of an inheritance dispute with his brother. Jesus deflects the request and instead directs a warning to the crowd about greed (πλεονεξίας) and the accumulation of possessions (12:13–15, 21). Jesus' growing conflict in the Lucan Travel Narrative is not only with the religious authorities but also with the crowd, many of whom remain unrepentant at his preaching and merit his epithet as an evil generation (11:29–32). It may be surmised that a significant portion of the crowd consists of the rich whom Jesus exhorts against greed and the accumulation of wealth because of their failure to practice almsgiving.[4]

---

4. Matera ("Jesus' Journey," 70) notes that "By the conclusion of this discourse

The unsavory character of the rich man in this parable is revealed through his interior monologue in which he deliberates about what to do with his bountiful harvest. His decision to store up the harvest rather than share any of the abundance with his neighbors, when viewed from a limited goods perspective, is an immoral one for it deprives others of what they need to subsist. Furthermore, his quotation of the proverb "rest, eat, drink, be merry!" (12:19) is an affront to God for it reflects the pursuit of hedonism without fear or expectation of divine judgment.[5] The structure of the parable contradicts the Deuteronomistic axiom that prosperity in one's lifetime proves that one is blessed by God, asserting instead that use of wealth is subject to God's judgment. Rather, the rich man is qualified by God as a fool, a curse that occasions immediate death because he failed to become rich toward God by practicing almsgiving. The normally more moderate attitude towards wealth in the "L" parables is suspended in this case.[6]

The Great Banquet (14:16–24)

Jesus relates the parable of the Great Banquet during a Sabbath dinner in the house of a leading Pharisee (τῶν ἀρχόντων τῶν Φαρισαίων), with lawyers and other Pharisees (τοὺς νομικοὺς καὶ Φαρισαίους) in attendance (14:1, 3). This is obviously a dinner for the social and religious elite whom Jesus calls to repentance. One of these rich guests utters a pious blessing about dining in the kingdom of God, to which Jesus responds not with a blessing but with this parable[7] that highlights their conflicting points of

---

[12:1b—13:9], the reader understands that both the crowd and the disciples need instruction in the use of possessions. The narrator, however, portrays the disciples as more receptive to Jesus' teaching while suggesting that the unrepentant crowd, now called hypocrites [in 12:56], is dangerously close to the point of view of its religious leaders."

5. Johnson, *Luke*, 199. On the accumulation of riches and divine judgment, see 1 *Enoch* 97:8–10.

6. Paffenroth (*According to L*, 123) states that "The possession of wealth is depicted negatively in the L pericopae only when it has obscured or overridden the character's other concerns, becoming the most important thing in his or her life." Such is the case in 12:16–20 and 16:19–31.

7. Jesus' teaching in Luke consistently subverts an elitist vision of the eschatological banquet and challenges the concrete social and economic arrangements affiliated with such a vision of kingdom and society. Luke employs such blessings to depict flawed forms of piety as a foil for Jesus' corrective teaching with regard to participation in the kingdom of God. The normal and expected response to the dinner guest's pious blessing is for Jesus to respond in kind with a blessing of his own. Frequently, however, Jesus rejects such piety and asserts an opposing view.

view about the correct use of wealth and the nature of the kingdom.[8] The parable achieves the effect of urging the rich to repent through almsgiving in the form of sharing of food with the most socially marginalized by depicting the inclusion of the stereotypical poor over the self-exclusion of the stereotypically rich.

The contrast in characterization between the rich and the poor in this parable is extreme. The originally invited guests are portrayed as the richest of the rich obsessed with consolidating their status in society through their unquenchable desire to accumulate wealth as an absentee landowner, an oxen trader, and a newlywed seeking economic and social advantage. Meanwhile, the replacement guests are portrayed as the poorest of the poor gathered from the peripheral streets and lanes of the city and the roads and hedges outside the city walls. The structure of the parable disorients and reverses the reader's expectations about who will be included in and excluded from participation in the eschatological banquet in the kingdom of God. Although the parable of the Great Banquet is not strictly speaking one of the special "L" parables, it nonetheless advocates the proper use of wealth and possessions for almsgiving as distribution of food to the hungry rather than complete renunciation of such. The figure of the rich banquet host, then, provides a positive model of the conversion and repentance espoused by Jesus in the Lucan Travel Narrative.

The Prodigal Son (15:11–32)

Jesus addresses the parable of the Prodigal Son to the Pharisees and scribes (οἵ τε Φαρισαῖοι καὶ οἱ γραμματεῖς) who grumble because he eats with tax collectors and sinners (πάντες οἱ τελῶναι καὶ οἱ ἁμαρτωλοί) and who were all drawing near to listen to his teaching (15:2).[9] In contrast to the religious elite and a significant portion of the crowds, Jesus' call to repentance finds a hearing among those considered ritually polluted by the leaders of Israel. There is no explicit exhortation to almsgiving, unless one considers the extension of compassion for the repentant sinner as a form of giving alms. This may well be what is intended as such unmerited compassion

---

8. Matera ("Jesus' Journey," 72) notes that "whereas the Pharisees view the kingdom as a banquet to which only the socially acceptable will be invited, Jesus views it as a banquet to which the poor, the lame, the blind and the crippled will be invited."

9. Matera (ibid., 72–73) observes ". . . Jesus' table fellowship with sinners signifies a break with the Pharisees and scribes who no longer invite him to dine with them."

involved the reincorporation of the sinner into the social and economic spheres of life. In any case, the parable may hearken back to 7:29–30 which previews the bifurcation among the people in response to the preaching of Jesus that has now become clearly defined at this point in the Lucan Travel Narrative:

> All the people who listened, including the tax collectors (οἱ τελῶ ναι), and who were baptized with the baptism of John, acknowledged the righteousness of God; but the Pharisees and the scholars of the law (οἱ Φαρισαῖοι καὶ οἱ νομικοί), who were not baptized by him, rejected the plan of God for themselves.

From an allegorical perspective, the parable of the Prodigal Son has to do with acknowledging God's (the father's) righteousness in extending compassion toward even the most egregious sinner (the younger son) who repents. The religious elite (the older son) cannot accept this and in so doing reject God's plan for their own salvation: they are to be considered dead and lost.[10]

The characters of both the younger son and the older son are revealed through their speeches. The younger son's interior monologue in 15:18–19 exhibits the proper attitude of the repentant sinner: "Father, I have sinned against heaven and against you. I no longer deserve to be called your son; treat me as you would treat one of your hired workers." The older son's rant against the father in 15:29–30 exhibits the attitude of those who refuse to repent: "Look, all these years I served you and not once did I disobey your orders; yet you never gave me even a young goat to feast on with my friends. But when your son returns who swallowed up your property with prostitutes, for him you slaughter the fattened calf." The parable's structure reverses the expected exclusion of the younger son to one of inclusion, and the expected inclusion of the older son to one of impending exclusion.

The Dishonest Steward (16:1–8)

The parable of the Dishonest Steward differs from the other φιλάργυροι parables as it is the only one that Jesus addresses to the disciples and as such should be taken as instruction rather than polemic. This perspective

---

10. This impression is strengthened by the emphasis on rejoicing over the repentance of sinners in the parables of the Lost Sheep in 15:7 ("I tell you, in just the same way there will be more joy in heaven over one sinner who repents than over ninety-nine righteous people who have no need of repentance") and the Lost Coin in 15:10 ("In just the same way, I tell you, there will be rejoicing among the angels of God over one sinner who repents").

is reinforced by the verses following the parable that teach the disciples to make friends for themselves with dishonest wealth through the practice of almsgiving and to be trustworthy in their financial dealings so as to be trusted with true wealth (16:9–12). Once again, an explicit link is made between almsgiving and one's fate in the afterlife.

The character of the dishonest steward is revealed through his interior monologue and his interactions with his master's debtors. The steward deliberates about how to secure his future now that he will lose his position and settles upon a clever strategy. In the little time that remains, he makes the rounds and writes off a portion of the debt each owed to the master. From an honor/shame perspective, the debtors would assume the steward is acting on his master's behalf and would praise the master for his generosity, thereby making it socially impossible for the master to punish the steward. It is this cleverness that the master praises. The parable teaches that almsgiving is a proper use of dishonest wealth to demonstrate repentance for one's own sins and to hold God honor bound to withhold punishment. The structure of the parable reverses the expected outcome of the steward's fate from one of punishment to one of adulation. A less radical attitude towards wealth predominates in this "L" parable since only a portion of the debt is written off.

The Rich Man and Lazarus (16:19–31)

Jesus addresses the parable of the Rich Man and Lazarus to the Pharisees, who in preceding verses are now described as those who love money (16:14), implying that they hate God, given the dichotomy set up by Jesus: "No servant can serve two masters. He will either hate one and love the other, or be devoted to one and despise the other. You cannot serve God and mammon" (16:13). As money-lovers and God-haters, the parable depicts the fate of such obstinate individuals who refuse to seek repentance through almsgiving as required by the Law and the Prophets. They will be excluded and tormented in the afterlife, while those they neglected will be included and comforted.

Both the characters of poor Lazarus and the rich man are depicted quite graphically, the former as utterly destitute and diseased, the latter as obscenely wealthy and hedonistic. However, it is the character of the rich man that is further revealed through his threefold dialogue with Abraham as one who is shameless and unrepentant even in death. The structure of the parable reverses the expected fates of the rich man and the poor man according to the Deuteronomisitic axiom concerning prosperity as the sign of God's blessing. As in the parable of the Rich Fool, the possession of wealth is depicted negatively in special "L" material only when it becomes the overriding concern of the character devoted to its exclusive consumption and accumulation.

The Pharisee and the Tax Collector (18:10–14)

Jesus addresses the parable of the Pharisee and the Tax Collector to "those who were convinced of their own righteousness and despised everyone else" (18:9). As such, it is directed in a summary way to all those who remain unrepentant at this concluding section of the Lucan Travel Narrative. While there are references to fasting and tithing, almsgiving is not mentioned.

The character of the Pharisee as a member of the social and religious elite, and as such a representative of all the unrepentant rich that Jesus has been attempting to persuade to repent, is depicted through the words of his self-aggrandizing prayer, revealing an elitist perspective that presumes superiority over the rest of humanity, whom he disparages as sinfully rapacious, unrighteous, and adulterous (ἅρπαγες, ἄδικοι, μοιχοί). Interestingly enough, the self-righteous prayer reveals his hypocrisy as these are the very sinful behaviors and attitudes that Jesus condemns among the Pharisees earlier on in the narrative.[11] They ignore Jesus' exhortation to give alms for repentance, to fear judgment, and love God (11:39–42). In contrast, the tax collector utters a simple prayer for mercy and is justified while the Pharisee is not. The structure of the parable calls into question who is really justified in God's eyes. The issue of the correct use of wealth is not directly addressed.

This short survey of these φιλάργυροι parables suggests that these seven parables form a coherent subset within the Lucan Travel Narrative that is geared toward persuading the rich to repentance. In summary: (A) Six of the seven parables are addressed by Jesus to one or more rich and unrepentant characters in the narrative (a lawyer, the crowd, Pharisees and lawyers, Pharisees and scribes, the Pharisees and all the unrepentant). (B) Four of the seven parables illustrate the need for repentance in the form of almsgiving or other merciful practice toward the needy (compassion toward a victim of violence,

---

11. See for example 11:39–42 where Jesus excoriates the Pharisees for their inner greed and wickedness (ἁρπαγῆς καὶ πονηρίας). Elsewhere, Jesus condemns their love of money (16:14) and alludes to their possibly adulterous behavior (16:16–18).

sharing of food with the hungry, forgiveness for the repentant sinner, remission of debt), while the other three illustrate the consequences of failing to do so (death, torment in the afterlife, non-justification). (C) All seven of these parables reveal the characters and interior dispositions of one or more of their actors through their speech (a rich yet compassionate Samaritan, a rich fool, a rich banquet host turned generous toward the poor, a repentant younger son and his unforgiving older brother, a clever steward, a heartless rich man, a self-righteous and hypocritical Pharisee). (D) The rhetorical structure of four of these parables guides the reader through an explicit threefold process of reversal composed of orientation, disorientation, and reorientation (the Good Samaritan, the Great Banquet, the Prodigal Son, the Rich Man and Lazarus) while the remaining three illustrate such reversal through an abbreviated process. (E) Six of these parables are special "L" parables that generally exhibit a less radical and less negative attitude toward wealth and the wealthy when compared with other material in the Gospel. None of these parables advocates the complete renunciation of wealth but rather models almsgiving and other assistance to the needy (the Good Samaritan, the Great Banquet, the Prodigal Son, the Dishonest Steward).

I now turn to a closer examination of how these φιλάργυροι parables achieve their purpose of persuading the rich to repentance through a set of four parabolic dynamics, that is, logical structures and strategies that move the reader from a vision of reality that is exclusive and elitist to a vision that is inclusive, egalitarian, and associated with Jesus' preaching about the kingdom of God.

PARABOLIC DYNAMICS IN LUCAN TRAVEL NARRATIVE PARABLES FOR THE REPENTANCE OF THE RICH

The contours of these φιλάργυροι parables may be further delimited by the following four shared parabolic dynamics, by which I mean narrative structures and strategies geared toward the persuasion of the rich to repentance. Φιλάργυροι parables (a) are fictional stories explicitly grounded in the social, political, economic, and cultural realities of human existence; (b) metaphorically propose to the imagination an alternate vision of reality associated with aspects of Jesus' proclamation of the kingdom of God; (c) challenge and subvert the established order by guiding the hearer/reader through a process of orientation, disorientation, and reorientation, and; (d) elicit new responses, value judgments, relationships, expectations, and attitudes adequate to the alternate kingdom of God vision of reality proposed. I will now explore each of these four shared parabolic dynamics in turn.

The Established Vision of Reality

The parables of Jesus, whether as originally spoken by Jesus himself or as reframed in the Gospel narratives, were proclaimed within the general historical context of the first-century Mediterranean world and as such convey a particular vision of the established order of reality. This is no less true regarding the subset of φιλάργυροι parables contained in the Lucan Travel Narrative identified above. However, the sense of realism is heightened in these seven parables so as to anchor them more explicitly in the realities of human existence. Although presented as fictional stories, they come across as depicting entirely plausible characters and events, at least at the outset.[12] Such realism mitigates the tendency to abstract from these parables universal theological doctrines and ethical principles divorced from any social context and devoid of any potential challenge to the *status quo*. Dramatic representation of human experience within an established vision of reality constitutes the first shared parabolic dynamic among the φιλάργυροι parables; namely, *parables are fictional stories explicitly grounded in the social, political, economic, and cultural realities of human existence*.

The realistic point of departure demonstrates the ultimate seriousness of the parable's subject. The initial emphasis on the realities of human existence, on everydayness, is intended to illuminate precisely those underlying human realities that are frequently hidden from more critical evaluation because of social custom or consensus and thus more resistant to potential modification. "The parable does not direct attention by its earthly imagery *away from* mundane existence, but *toward* it. The realism of the parable is not merely a device. Everydayness is ingredient [*sic*] in the parable because everydayness constitutes the locus of the parable's intentionality."[13]

The vision of the established order addressed in the parables is a socially constructed reality, one that functions as a kind of interpretive grid

---

12. Ricoeur ("Biblical Hermeneutics," 115) states: "The parables tell stories that could have happened or without a doubt have happened, but it is this realism of situations, characters, and plots that precisely heightens the eccentricity of the modes of behavior to which the Kingdom of heaven is compared."

13. Funk, *Language*, 156. Author's emphases.

against which to understand events and persons in the world. As in every human society of every time and place, the social world conditions both how societies as a whole structure their world externally, through objective realities such as institutions with their corresponding roles and identities, and how individuals internalize their own subjective existence and behavior within that particular society through the process of socialization. Normally, the social world is self-legitimizing by virtue of its "objective facticity," that is, by the very fact of its existence. The social world is the taken-for-granted, unreflected-upon understanding of the way things are.[14] The validity of the established order comes into question only with the occurrence of phenomena unexplainable within the current framework or by way of overt challenge from individuals or groups. When this happens, additional legitimizations, especially religious legitimizations, become necessary to buttress and further justify the existing social order against collapse.[15] "Religious legitimizations purport to relate the humanly defined reality to ultimate, universal and sacred reality. The inherently precarious and transitory constructions of human activity are thus given the semblance of ultimate security and permanence."[16]

Bruce Malina identifies three truisms that are relevant for understanding the general historical context of the first-century Mediterranean social world: that all goods are limited and can only be increased at the expense of others, that no one goes without the things necessary for basic human subsistence, and that the rich person is inherently evil. In a limited goods society, the presumption is that a rich person, or that person's ancestors, must have taken from others who now have less. Furthermore, when the amassing of wealth becomes an end in itself, the person dedicated to such behavior must be evil since he or she deprives others from meeting their needs for human living. In this perspective, to state that the rich person is necessarily evil is axiomatic.[17]

---

14. Berger, *Sacred Canopy*, 19–21. For a more in-depth discussion of society as both an objective reality and a subjective reality, see further Berger and Luckmann, *Social Construction*.

15. Ibid., 29–31. Religion is the most effective tool of legitimization in that it associates the precarious social world with the stability of ultimate reality. In other words, that which is essentially arbitrary and human (institutions, roles, identities) is invested with an aura of inevitability and permanence through its projection onto the cosmic and divine plane of existence.

16. Ibid., 35–36.

17. Malina, *Social Gospel of Jesus*, 103–9.

The initial points of departure in each of the seven φιλάργυροι parables present plausible situations and characters that resonate with real world experience from the perspective of the poor. From this established vision of reality, the poor are victims of neglect, violence, destitution, and even utter destruction at the hands of the rich who are portrayed stereotypically as consumed with maintaining or increasing their own social status and wealth. The social and religious elite priest and Levite fail to demonstrate basic human compassion for the half-dead robbery victim at the side of the road. A rich man hordes a bountiful harvest for himself rather than even consider the needs of his hungry neighbors. Another rich man prepares a great banquet for his rich peers, intended to enhance his honor and position among his friends. The younger son of a rich man severs family ties by amassing his inheritance. A rich man confronts his steward for mismanaging property, while indifferent to the plight of his debtors. A rich man is finely attired for his daily banquets while unmoved by the exposed poor man dying of hunger lying at his gate. The Pharisee's self-righteous prayer to God betrays his disdain for the rest of humanity. Thus, the established vision of reality reflected in these parables is a world in which the rich willfully neglect and oppress the helpless poor for their own personal gain, and proudly consider themselves favored by God in the process.

The point of departure for φιλάργυροι parables is the real literal world of everydayness. It orients the reader in the social, political, economic, and cultural realities of human existence. The characters and their behaviors are initially plausible, albeit at times drawn hyperbolically to enhance and intensify their realism.[18] By so intensifying the focus on the realities of the established order, these parables prepare the reader to confront the possibilities of an alternate vision of reality by way of dramatic contrast.

An Alternate Vision of Reality

A second shared parabolic dynamic among φιλάργυροι parables is that they *metaphorically propose to the imagination an alternate vision of reality associated with aspects of Jesus' proclamation of the kingdom of God.* The metaphorical quality of these parables refers to the analogy drawn in narrative form between two different visions of reality, the actual established order and a potential alternate vision. These two distinct but not entirely dissimilar elements are juxtaposed in such a way as to spark the

18. Funk, *Language*, 161.

imagination with new insights into the actual situation described and to propose the inauguration of an alternate vision of reality that cannot be conveyed through normal discursive speech.[19]

The effectiveness of parables as metaphors lies in their power to provoke what Robert Funk describes as "imaginative shock." Whereas a simile merely illustrates or clarifies a reality already acknowledged, a metaphor is creative of new meaning. Parables as metaphors insinuate new meanings and new realities as yet unimagined or at least unrealized. The interpretive grid of the established order, the objective facticity of the social world, is peeled back as it were, and a new interpretive grid is superimposed to re-order the realities and priorities of human existence. The element of shock lies in this subversive, even destructive, potential: "Metaphor shatters the conventions of predication in the interests of a new vision, one which grasps the 'thing' in relation to a new 'field,' and thus in relation to a fresh experience of reality. Metaphor does not illustrate this or that idea; it abuses ideas with their propensity for censoring sight."[20]

Whether explicit or implied, the new "field" within which the parables of Jesus project human reality, the new interpretive grid proposed to the imagination, is the symbol of the kingdom of God. A symbol, as generally defined by Philip Wheelwright, "is a relatively stable and repeatable element of perceptual experience, standing for some larger meaning or set of meanings which cannot be given, or not fully given, in perceptual experience itself."[21] A symbol may be either a steno-symbol, possessing a one-to-one relationship to that which it represents, or a tensive symbol, possessing a set of meanings that can neither be exhausted nor adequately expressed by any one referent.[22]

The alternate vision of reality referred to in the parables of Jesus is encapsulated by the tensive symbol of the kingdom of God. As a tensive symbol, it evokes a whole set of meanings rooted in Jewish myth and tradition. It combines mythical elements of God acting as king in the creation of the world and historical elements of God's acts of salvation on behalf of a particular people.[23] But neither can it be completely exhausted or de-

---

19. Ibid., 136. See also Black, *Models and Metaphors*, 237.
20. Funk, *Language*, 139.
21. Wheelwright, *Metaphor and Reality*, 92.
22. Ibid., 93–96.
23. Perrin, *Language of the Kingdom*, 15–22, 32. Perrin, however, clarifies that in ancient Jewish apocalyptic, the kingdom of God was understood predominately as a

fined. Rather, as a high context symbol from a high context society, it is sketchy and impressionistic, leaving much to the imagination and common knowledge. It assumes a way of perceiving reality and appropriate behavior that is socially conditioned. Whereas low context symbols from low context societies spell out everything in much detail, reference to the kingdom of God in Jesus' proclamation evokes social realities with wide-ranging ramifications understood by all persons in first-century Jewish society without the need to enumerate what these were.[24] The enduring power of Jesus' parables rests precisely in their continuing ability to stimulate and shock the human imagination into entertaining new ways of structuring society and engendering new ways of relating to the world.

In the φιλάργυροι parables, an element of imaginative shock is the catalyst that challenges the reader to reevaluate the established vision of reality in order to contemplate embracing a new reality. An outsider, a Samaritan, is compassionate toward a roadside victim. A rich man with a bountiful harvest is not blessed but qualified by God as a fool. A rich man's banquet is enjoyed by the poor, crippled, blind, and lame. A rich father is compassionate toward his younger son who severed family ties and squandered his inheritance. A dishonest steward uses his master's wealth to win friends for himself, not among the rich, but among the poor. A rich man unexpectedly finds himself tormented in Hades while a poor man is comforted in Abraham's bosom. The self-righteous and observant Pharisee leaves the temple unjustified while the sinner who asks for mercy goes home justified.

Two different visions of reality are depicted in Jesus' proclamation of these φιλάργυροι parables, the actual established order and a potential alternate vision of reality evoked by the tensive symbol of the kingdom of God. One is known more concretely and experientially, the other only impressionistically and intuitively. The imaginative shock produced by this juxtaposition is intended to persuade the reader to reject one reality and embrace another, reordering the priorities of human existence in light of the kingdom proclamation.

---

steno-symbol in light of its use to express the expectation that God would intervene in the course of a particular war.

24. Malina, *Social Gospel of Jesus*, 2–3.

Challenge and Subversion of the Established Order

A third shared parabolic dynamic among the φιλάργυροι parables is that they *challenge and subvert the established order by guiding the hearer/reader through a process of orientation, disorientation, and reorientation.* In the parable's first movement the reader is oriented to the established order of reality, more precisely to some familiar aspect of the social, political, economic, or cultural world of the reader. This orientation may focus the reader's attention upon the aspect in question by way of hyperbolic portrayal of central characters, but it is a generally plausible presentation. In the parable's second movement, the reader is abruptly disoriented as the expected dynamics of the world of common experience break down. The parable presents the reader with an alternate vision of reality where characters do not behave as they normally do and expected outcomes are unfulfilled. In the parable's third movement, the reader is reoriented to that new vision of reality. Objective reality is viewed from an alternate perspective, one associated with dimensions of Jesus' proclamation of the kingdom of God. The parable depicts characters that must conform to new criteria for value judgments and human relationships.

The implied presumption behind these parables, then, is that the established reality is in some way defective and requires challenge and subversion in order to conform more closely to the divinely ordained order encapsulated by the symbol of the kingdom of God. Paul Ricoeur describes how parables achieve this rhetorical effect through the vehicle of metaphorical language. In science, a model "is essentially a heuristic instrument that seeks, by means of fiction, to break down an inadequate interpretation and to lay the way for a new, more adequate interpretation."[25] Parables function in much the same way as theoretical models do, whereby the original is described in different language without actually being constructed in the physical world. The model functions as a mnemonic device that provides the user with an imaginary object that is more familiar, can be viewed conceptually from different perspectives, and is full of implications for apprehending the original.[26] A

---

25. Ricoeur, *Rule of Metaphor*, 240. Ricoeur is dependent upon the work of Black, *Models and Metaphors* for his description of models and Hesse, *Models and Analogies* for her explanation that a model is an instrument of redescription.

26. Ricoeur, *Rule of Metaphor*, 241. Black (*Models and Metaphors*, 219–43) describes three kinds of models based upon makeup and function: a scale model (a reproduction of an original that is either too small or too large, intended to demonstrate how something looks, how it works, and what laws govern it); an analogue model (a reproduction of an

parable functions as a theoretical model for the conceptually more complex reality encapsulated by the kingdom of God symbol:

> The great advantage of this rapprochement is to emphasize the referential claim of the figurative narratives, and therefore their existential-referential dimension. If a model is a heuristic device which serves to break up a previously inadequate description and to blaze a trail toward a new, more adequate description, the metaphor comes closest to this heuristic function when the metaphorical process is channeled by a fictional narrative. Then it displays the same power of *connecting fiction and redescription*.[27]

Most of the seven φιλάργυροι parables under consideration here possess this three-fold structure of orientation, disorientation, and reorientation, providing a kind of theoretical model for embracing one or more aspects of the kingdom proclamation. Readers are to imitate the compassion of the Samaritan, not the indifference of the priest and Levite. The compassionate father welcomes back the son who strays despite his having severed family ties and squandered his inheritance. God frowns upon the self-righteousness of the Pharisee but favors the repentant sinner. Likewise, these parables also provide positive depictions of what repentance among the rich might look like and the negative consequences of remaining unrepentant. The rich are not to horde and amass their wealth. The rich are to share their banquets with the poor and hungry instead of engaging in conspicuous consumption with their peers. Reduction of debt can win friends among the poor. The unrepentant rich who fail to act with compassion as taught by Moses and the prophets risk eternal exclusion and torment in the afterlife.

Responses Adequate to the Alternate Vision of Reality

Φιλάργυροι parables *require a response from their readers in the form of abandoning values and behaviors from the established vision of reality in favor of embracing the new values, relationships, expectations, and attitudes espoused in response to Jesus' proclamation of the kingdom.* Parables are not merely vehicles for expressing theological and ethical doctrine. Jülicher understood parables as possessing one moral point of the broadest possible application. Jeremias contended that the one point of the parable must be

---

original in a different medium that functions to represent internal structural relationships), and; a theoretical model (an immaterial, conceptual representation of an original).

27. Ricoeur, "Biblical Hermeneutics," 95. (Author's emphasis).

related to the historical context of Jesus' ministry in which it was uttered, so that the point is eschatological.[28] However, to reduce the significance of a parable to one moral or eschatological point it to eviscerate the parable of its subversive propensity to generate new visions of reality and new ways of structuring human society.

Nor are parables merely a tool for social analysis. Malina examines what sort of social problems Jesus' proclamation of the kingdom of God addressed. He contends that Jesus' proclamation of the kingdom was not metaphorical but political, intended to address the failure of elite patrons to fulfill their obligations toward their non-elite clients. Overcoming the collapse of the dysfunctional patronage system, the establishment of a theocracy promises restoration of the God of Israel as divine patron.[29] Similarly, William Herzog analyzes the parables and kingdom language from the viewpoint of the historical Jesus. The parables dealt with political and social issues and were pedagogical tools that subverted oppressive reality.[30]

Parables are both temporally open ended, their generative ability not limited to any historical era, as well as polyvalent, stimulating the imagination to conceive of a multiplicity of applications in the real world. The challenge is to articulate how the alternate vision of reality expressed in the parables functions in a particular gospel narrative and for the modern reader.

Taken alone, an individual parable may convey this or that aspect of the alternate reality of the kingdom. However, Jesus' parables more effectively convey their rhetorical purpose of "reorientation by disorientation"[31] when viewed as a collection that is mutually reinforcing in the direction of its rhetorical thrust. The evangelist also influences the thrust of individual parables by his selection, redaction, and framing of parables within a wider narrative framework. Such is the case with the seven φιλάργυροι parables in the Lucan Travel Narrative identified here. Taken together, these parables subvert the values of the established reality wherein wealth and status is prized over the welfare of the poor. The rich and self-righteous are not blessed in God's eyes. Rather they are in danger of exclusion from the kingdom unless they reorient their values and relationships to benefit the poor by concrete actions of almsgiving and compassion.

---

28. Funk, *Language*, 147–49.
29. Malina, *Social Gospel of Jesus*, 1, 33–35.
30. Herzog, *Subversive Speech*.
31. Ibid., 120, 126.

THE TEXT OF THE PARABLE OF THE RICH MAN AND LAZARUS

Having isolated the subset of seven φιλάργυροι parables in the Lucan Travel Narrative that exhibit a certain affinity with regard to persuading the rich to repentance and having examined the four shared parabolic dynamics by which these parables achieve their purpose, we are now in a position to introduce the text of the parable of the Rich Man and Lazarus. This section will present an original translation of the parable and discuss the limited number of significant textual variants that appear in the tradition. Thereafter, a brief preliminary exegetical presentation will serve to articulate the threefold structure of orientation/disorientation/reorientation and to illustrate by concrete example how the four parabolic dynamics achieve their purpose of persuading the rich to repentance. The brief exegetical presentation will also introduce some of the social-science issues that will be examined in more detail in chapters 3 and 4.

Translation

The following is my own translation of the parable of the Rich Man and Lazarus, with careful attention to the graphic contrasts suggested by the text itself. For the sake of illustration, I present this translation according to the threefold internal structure of orientation, disorientation, and reorientation described as the third parabolic dynamic discussed above.

Orientation: Earthly Life

19 There was a rich man
   who was clothed in a purple robe and fine linen garments
   and who feasted sumptuously every day.
20 There was also a poor man named Lazarus
   who lay at his gate, was covered with sores,
21 and who yearned to be fed with whatever fell from the rich man's table;
   moreover, dogs came and licked his sores.

Tormented in Hades

Disorientation: Death

> 22 The poor man died
> and was carried away by the angels to Abraham's bosom;
> the rich man also died
> and was buried.
>
> 23 Tormented in Hades, he raised his eyes
> and saw Abraham from afar
> and Lazarus at his bosom.

Reorientation: Afterlife and Reversal

> 24 He cried out, "Father Abraham, have mercy on me!
> Send Lazarus to dip the tip of his finger in water and cool my tongue,
> because I am tormented in these flames!"
>
> 25 Abraham replied, "My child,
> remember that you received good fortune in your lifetime
> while Lazarus received only misfortune in his;
> now he is comforted here
> while you are tormented.
>
> 26 Moreover, a great chasm is established between you and us,
> so that those who would want to cross over from here to you cannot do so,
> nor can anyone from there cross over to us."
>
> 27 So he said, "Then I beg you, Father,
> send him to my father's house, 28 for I have five brothers, that he may warn them,
> lest they also come to this place of torment!"
>
> 29 Abraham replied,
> "They have Moses and the prophets;
> let them listen to them."
>
> 30 So he said, "No, Father Abraham!
> Certainly if someone from the dead would go to them, they will repent!"

31 Abraham replied,
"If they will not listen to Moses and the prophets,
then they will not be persuaded even if someone rises from the dead."

Significant Textual Variants

Although nearly every verse of this parable contains at least one textual variant, most consist of orthographic differences, transpositions, and substitutions that would not alter the parable's meaning or interpretation to any significant degree. Indeed the text of this parable is relatively stable, with some 93 percent of the text regarded as fully established, the remaining 7 percent due to one addition and seven insertions/omissions.[32] Nonetheless, I will highlight eight of the textual variants noted in the twenty-seventh revised edition of Nestle-Aland *Novum Testamentum Graece*[33] given the antiquity of their witnesses, their relevance for signaling probable Lucan redaction, or their generally curious nature.

1. After the introductory Ἄνθρωπος δέ τις ἦν πλούσιος in v. 19, a significant witness inserts the phrase ὀνόματι Νευης. This variant is noteworthy insofar as it is found in P^{75}, the oldest Greek text of Luke dating to the third century, but it is absent from other witnesses. Joseph A. Fitzmyer notes that the meaning of the name itself "is unintelligible and is probably a shortened form of *Nineues*, which is also found in the ancient Sahidic version. . . ."[34] Suffice it to say that this variant likely represents an early attempt to provide the rich man with a name[35] and supply a parallel construction with the following verse, wherein the poor man is identified by his proper name: πτωχὸς δέ τις ὀνόματι Λάζαρος.

---

32. Robinson, "Rich Man and Lazarus," 96–110.
33. Nestle and Aland eds., *Novum Testamentum Graece*.
34. Fitzmyer, *According to Luke*, 1130. Fitzmyer explains the common misinterpretation of the Latin Vulgate phrase "*Homo quidam erat dives*," whereby the adjective *dives* is mistaken for the rich man's name "Dives."
35. B. M. Metzger (*Textual Commentary*, 140) states: "It was probably *horror vacui* that prompted more than one copyist to provide a name for the anonymous Rich Man. In Egypt the tradition that his name was Nineveh is incorporated in the Sahidic version, and seems to be reflected also in P^{75}, which reads πλούσιος ὀνόματι Νευης (probably a scribal error for Νινευης)." The third century pseudo-Cyprianic treatise *De pascha computus* contains the name Phineas, perhaps because of the association of Eleazar and Phinehas in Num 25:7, 11.

Tormented in Hades

2. In v. 21, some ancient witnesses[36] read τῶν ψιχίων after the first ἀπό in the phrase ἀπὸ τῶν πιπτόντων ἀπὸ τῆς τραπέζης τοῦ πλουσίου. This probably represents a conflation with Matt 15:27 in which the same phrase is employed by the Canaanite woman in her stinging rejoinder to Jesus' initial refusal to heal her daughter.

3. In v. 21, a few witnesses[37] read καὶ οὐδεὶς ἐδίδου αὐτῷ after the end of the previous phrase. Once again, this reading probably represents a scribal expansion, this time with Luke 15:16 in reference to the prodigal son's utter destitution.

4. In some witnesses,[38] a reading exists in which the phrase ἐν τῷ ᾅδῃ from v. 23 is appended to the end of v. 22 without the conjunction καί. The result is a rather awkward reading which would nonsensically have the rich man buried in Hades. Bruce M. Metzger notes: "Considering the weight of the evidence supporting καί as well as the style of Luke who generally avoids asyndeton, the presence of καί before ἐν seems to be assured."[39] The phrase properly belongs to v. 23 where it introduces the location of the rich man after his death in counterdistinction to Lazarus' location at Abraham's bosom.

5. At the end of v. 23, some witnesses[40] read ἀναπαυόμενον after the phrase Λάζαρον ἐν τοῖς κόλποις αὐτοῦ. A possible connotation of Lazarus' "resting" at Abraham's bosom is that of reclining at a formal banquet, perhaps the eschatological banquet, in which case the participle would then not seem out of place. The addition of ἀναπαυόμενον would have served to make the banquet association more explicit.

6. The variant readings in v. 30 are particularly important in that they evince probable scribal revision of the text in order to emphasize the parable's association with the themes of Jesus' resurrection and persuasion of the rich to repent. The second half of v. 30 reads ἀλλ' ἐάν τις ἀπὸ νεκρῶν πορευθῇ πρὸς αὐτοὺς μετανοήσουσιν. Significantly, P^{75} reads τις ἀπὸ νεκρῶν ἐγερθῇ whereas ℵ reads τις ἀπὸ νεκρῶν ἀναστῇ. Many of the best manuscripts contain the verb πορευθῇ,[41] and

36. ℵ² A (D: -χων) W Θ Ψ $f^{(1),13}$ 33 $\mathcal{M}$ lat sy^{p,h} sa^{ms} bo^{pt}.
37. f^{13} pc 1 vg^{cl}.
38. ℵ* lat; Marcion.
39. B. M. Metzger, *Textual Commentary*, 141.
40. D Θ l 2211 it.
41. Fitzmyer, *According to Luke*, 1134.

The Parable of the Rich Man and Lazarus

this appears consistent with what the original reading may have been. The rich man is attempting to argue his point with Abraham that if someone would go to his brothers from the dead (τις ἀπὸ νεκρῶν πορευθῇ πρὸς αὐτούς), namely, by means of a vision or dream, they will repent. Arland Hultgren emphasizes that the concept of visitors from the dead contacting the living is not unknown in the Scriptural tradition and thus is not dependent upon post-resurrection Christian imagery.[42] Therefore, both the ℵ reading ἀναστῇ and the P^{75} reading ἐγερθῇ are most likely scribal attempts to relate the parable to the theme of Jesus' resurrection.

7. Verse 31 manifests certain signs of Lucan redaction relating the parable to the themes of Jesus' resurrection and of the persuasion of the rich to repent. With regard to the theme of Jesus' resurrection, the second half of v. 31 reads οὐδ' ἐάν τις ἐκ νεκρῶν ἀναστῇ πεισθήσονται. The reading in P^{75} is τις ἐκ νεκρῶν ἐγερθῇ while another reading in W is τις ἐκ νεκρῶν ἀπέλθῃ. Still another reading in D presents a conflation of versions: τις ἐκ νεκρῶν ἀναστῇ καὶ ἀπέλθῃ πρὸς αὐτούς. This variety of renderings among P^{75}, W, and D suggests that the change from τις ἀπὸ νεκρῶν πορευθῇ in v. 30 to τις ἐκ νεκρῶν ἀναστῇ in v. 31 is evidence of Luke's redactional hand, drawing the interpretation of the parable in the direction of intentional allusion to Jesus' resurrection.

8. With regard to the theme of the persuasion of the rich to repent, the end of v. 31 reads οὐδ' ἐάν τις ἐκ νεκρῶν ἀναστῇ πεισθήσονται. The concluding verb πεισθήσονται echoes the theme of persuasion of the rich to repent emphasized throughout Luke-Acts. Some witnesses[43] read πιστεύσουσιν, however πεισθήσονται is clearly preferred. The rich man's insistence on the potential for repentance in v. 30 (μετανοήσουσιν) and Abraham's denial of such potential in v. 31 (οὐδ' ἐάν τις ἐκ νεκρῶν ἀναστῇ πεισθήσονται) is suggestive of Lucan redactional activity and consistent with the failure of the rich to repent related in the rest of Luke-Acts.

---

42. Hultgren (*Parables of Jesus*, 114) observes: "That a person from the realm of the dead would visit the brothers seems at first sight to depend on post-Easter Christian imagery. But the motif is older than Christianity. Various texts speak of the dead contacting the living, especially through dreams." See especially 1 Sam 28:6–19; 2 Kgs 21:6; Isa 8:19 in this regard.

43. D lat sy[s.c.p]; Ir[lat].

Tormented in Hades

Structure and Brief Exegetical Notes

The parable of the Rich Man and Lazarus presents a clear threefold structure that conforms to the rhetorical pattern of orientation, disorientation, and reorientation, guiding the reader from the earthly life, through death, and to the afterlife. The parable is to be understood as one unit with three movements.

Orientation: Earthly Life

Rich Man's Life (v. 19)

Poor Man's Life (vv. 20–21a)

Disjunctive note on wild dogs (v. 21b)

Disorientation: Death

Poor Man's Death (v. 22a)

Rich Man's Death (v. 22b)

Disjunctive note on reversal (v. 23)

Reorientation: Afterlife

Rich Man's first request (v. 24)

Abraham's first denial (vv. 25–26)

Rich Man's second request (vv. 27–28)

Abraham's second denial (v. 29)

Rich Man's third request (v. 30)

Abraham's third denial (v. 31)

The purpose of the brief exegetical notes that follow is to illustrate how the four parabolic dynamics discussed above, while relevant for each of the seven φιλάργυροι parables in the Lucan Travel Narrative, function in this particular parable to persuade the rich to repent. Some insights from the social-science perspective will also be introduced, along with some comments on characterization and narrative context. A more comprehensive exegetical presentation will follow our socio-narratological analysis of the parable of the Rich Man and Lazarus in chapter 4.

Orientation: Earthly Life

The first subdivision of the parable, Earthly Life, consists of vv. 19–21. The rich man described in v. 19 is starkly contrasted with the poor man who is identified in v. 20. The social and economic intensifiers of the rich man's clothing (purple robe and fine linen garments) are contrasted with the poor man's absence of clothing (covered with sores). The rich man's abundance of food (feasted sumptuously every day) is contrasted with the poor man's complete lack of food (yearned to be fed with whatever fell from the rich man's table). Thus, the contrast is based upon the primary social and economic indicators of clothing and food.

Verse 19: The introductory formula Ἄνθρωπος τις occurs only in the Lucan writings of the NT and suggests Lucan redaction.[44] The person referred to is identified as rich (πλούσιος), belonging to the privileged urban elite class. This identification is twice intensified in the description of his imported clothing (πορφύραν καὶ βύσσον) and his sumptuous feasting on a daily basis (εὐφραινόμενος καθ' ἡμέραν λαμπρῶς).[45] The rich man's clothing consists of a purple robe of fine wool dyed with imported Phoenician purple and fine linen garments imported from Egypt,[46] connoting exceedingly rich or even royal status. His feasting implies not only a surplus of food but exquisite banquets of conspicuous consumption with members of his exclusive social clique. Luke criticizes such elite sociability as self-serving, functioning to consolidate the power, status, and honor of the elite class in society:

> Underlying the criticism of the "merrymaking" of the rich was the assumption that wealth acquired by [the] rich was never shared with the common folk of the village, but circulated only among themselves. Thus, the inequality that existed in the first place was

---

44. See Luke 10:30; 12:16; 14:2, 16; 15:11; 16:1, 19; 19:12; 20:9; Acts 9:33. "[T]he use of *anthrōpos/anēr* with indef. *tis* is exclusive to Luke among the evangelists; both should be reckoned as part of his own style." Fitzmyer, *According to Luke*, 886.

45. The detail of feasting sumptuously every day (καθ' ἡμέραν) may be an instance of Lucan redaction. Luke has a tendency to "upsize" meals in his Gospel. This phenomenon is best seen in the parable of the Great Banquet when compared with its parallels in Matthew and *Thomas*.

46. Fitzmyer, *According to Luke*, 1130–31.

emphasized by the way in which the rich spent their wealth: not for the common good, but to protect their own position as a group over and against the needy people of the village.⁴⁷

Verses 20–21a: The poor man is described by employing the same narrative structure as that used to describe the rich man, providing a stark contrast between the two characters. While the poor man is described as poor (πτωχός), this identification is twice intensified in the description of his implied lack of clothing by his visible sores (εἱλκωμένος) and lack of food (ἐπιθυμῶν χορτασθῆναι), so that he might be understood as exceedingly poor, even destitute. The poor man's virtual nakedness can be surmised from his visibly being covered with sores. Such nakedness is shameless and marks the poor man as an outsider, demonized by society.⁴⁸ He yearns to be fed; the verb used here (χορτασθῆναι) connotes the feeding of hungry animals and is used by Luke on other occasions (6:21; 9:17; 15:16). The description of the poor man's situation, then, is literally dehumanizing.⁴⁹ Thus, the rich man of the parable is portrayed as an exceedingly rich member of the ruling urban elite, the poor man as an exceedingly poor member of the marginalized and outcast.

Verse 21b: There is more to the narrative detail (οἱ κύνες ἐρχόμενοι ἐπέλειχον τὰ ἕλκη αὐτοῦ) than initially meets the eye. The dogs are neither friendly companions, nor do they provide comfort by licking the poor man's sores. Rather, they are wild scavengers roaming the city streets "that detect and taste the 'fresh meat' that the sores on Lazarus would represent to them. They wait for his death."⁵⁰ The dogs foreshadow the imminence of the poor man's death that takes place immediately in the next verse.

---

47. Moxnes, *Economy of the Kingdom*, 89–90. The social-science model of meals and table-fellowship described by Neyrey, "Ceremonies," 361–87, is particularly helpful in this regard.

48. Moxnes, *Economy of the Kingdom*, 90–93. Compare Luke 10:30.

49. The poor man is identified by the name of Lazarus, meaning "God has helped," a fitting name for one not helped by his fellow human beings (Fitzmyer, *According to Luke*, 1131). Bretherton ("Lazarus of Bethany," 169–73) goes too far in suggesting that the Lazarus of the parable and the Lazarus in John 11 are one in the same. He even proposes that Lazarus of Bethany was not really dead but was in a state of suspended animation. The parable, he suggests, is the result of Lazarus' recollections during his near-death experience, which he subsequently relates to Jesus.

50. Hultgren, *Parables of Jesus*, 112. See 1 Kgs 14:11; 16:4; 21:24 for examples of dogs consuming the bodies of the dead, in this case, the bodies of enemies.

The Parable of the Rich Man and Lazarus

Disorientation: Death

The second subdivision of the parable, Death, consists of vv. 22–23. Here the rich man and the poor man are mentioned in inverted order. The poor man dies and no mention is made of any burial, emphasizing his poverty and isolation. The rich man also dies and is properly buried, presumably with the ceremony and fanfare befitting his socio-economic status. Verse 23, however, introduces the disorienting element of revealing that the dead rich man is tormented in Hades while the dead poor man is resting at Abraham's bosom. This abrupt description disorients the hearer from the expected resolution of the narrative.

Verse 22: Both men die while engaged in the activities that typified their lives. The poor man dies while still yearning to be fed at the rich man's gate. No mention is made of a proper burial,[51] and indeed it might even be surmised that the wild dogs performed their gruesome function of consuming his body. The narrative detail about the poor man being "carried away by angels" is curious in that such a belief does not occur in Jewish writings before the mid-second century.[52] In contrast, the rich man dies while feasting sumptuously, and is most likely buried with all the ceremony befitting his status.

Verse 23: To this point, the parable affirms the experiential reality of its hearers in terms of expectations regarding the behavior and respective fates of the rich and the poor. An abrupt and startling element of disorientation is introduced, however, when the poor man is depicted at Abraham's bosom and the rich man tormented in Hades. The parable begins to undermine conventional wisdom.

The portrayal of Lazarus at Abraham's bosom after death (Λάζαρον ἐν τοῖς κόλποις αὐτοῦ) has many possible associations. It may be a development of the OT idea of sleeping with one's ancestors (e.g., 1 Kgs 1:21; 2:10; 11:21; 4 Macc 13:17), or the designation of a place of honor to the right of the host at a banquet (ἐν τῷ κόλπῳ τοῦ Ἰησοῦ—John 13:23), or an association of

---

51. Scott (*Hear Then the Parable*, 152) comments that the lack of a decent burial constituted a scandal and a curse. It was thought that by depriving someone of a proper burial one could deprive someone of the resurrection or the afterlife.

52. Fitzmyer, *According to Luke*, 1132. Hultgren (*Parables of Jesus*, 113) suggests the phrase evokes "the taking of Enoch to heaven by God (Gen 5:24) and the taking of Elijah to heaven in a whirlwind (2 Kgs 2:11)." Alternately, it may be a euphemism used to describe those left unburied and eaten by dogs, birds, or other wild animals.

intimacy (ὁ ὢν εἰς τὸν κόλπον τοῦ πατρός—John 1:18).[53] The banquet association should be favored because of the poor man's former exclusion from such in earthly life. This is consistent with the theme of reversal, in which case the figurative tables have been turned on the rich man.

The rich man finds himself tormented in Hades (ἐν τῷ ᾅδῃ ἐπάρας τοὺς ὀφθαλμοὺς αὐτοῦ, ὑπάρχων ἐν βασάνοις) and sees Lazarus at Abraham's bosom. Elsewhere in Luke, Hades appears in the context of unwillingness to repent and judgment (Luke 10:13–15).

Reorientation: Afterlife

The third and final subdivision of the parable, Afterlife, consists of a series of three dialogical interchanges between the rich man and Abraham in vv. 24–31, while Lazarus remains silent. The three requests (vv. 24, 27–28, and 30) are crucial for the narrative development of the rich man's character. Similarly, Abraham's negative replies to each of the rich man's requests (vv. 25–26, 29, and 31) emphasize the reversal of fortunes that has occurred and the permanency of that reversal. This series of three interchanges between the rich man and Abraham is thus properly understood as one integral subunit of one unified parable.

Verse 24: The rich man pleads for mercy from Abraham, invoking God's promise (Gen 12:1–3/Luke 1:73) and his privileged status as a child of Abraham. The rich man's first request for water has less to do with physical thirst, although this is a standard torment in Hades, than with relief from mental anguish. The rich man is denied the usual drink from the River Lethe (the River of Forgetfulness), and so is doomed to remember his past life of luxury and opulence.[54] This interpretation of the first request is further supported by the use of the verb which denotes mental anguish (ὀδυνῶμαι)[55] and Abraham's negative response indicating that he must remember the good fortune of his lifetime (μνήσθητι ὅτι ἀπέλαβες τὰ ἀγαθά σου ἐν τῇ ζωῇ σου).

---

53. Fitzmyer, *According to Luke*, 1132.

54. See for example Lucian of Samosata's *Cataplus*, along with English translation, in Harmon, *Lucian*, 2.1–57.

55. This verb is used exclusively by Luke in the NT—in Luke 2:48, here in 16:24, 25, and in Acts 20:38—to describe intense anxiety, mental anguish, and sorrow (Fitzmyer, *According to Luke*, 443).

Verses 25–26: Abraham acknowledges the rich man as a descendant (τέκνον), yet denies his first request by reaffirming that he must be tormented by the memory of his lifetime of good fortune. No explicit criteria of judgment are supplied for the rich man's condemnation. This is reminiscent of the beatitudes and curses in Luke 6 that simply states the fact of the reversal. Perhaps no explicit criteria are necessary from the perspective of the poor, as the stereotype in societies of limited goods is that people who are rich became so at the expense of others. Bruce Malina makes this stereotype of the rich explicit:

> they became rich as the result of their own covetousness, or greed, or that of their ancestors. For typical of the rich is the amassing of surplus, of having more than enough and more than others. Significantly, one was presumed to have become rich by depriving others, defrauding and eliminating others, prospering by having others become wretched, pitiable, ill, blind, and naked.[56]

We may presume at this point that Lazarus has drunk the water from the River Lethe, and so has no remembrance of his past life of utter misery and is enjoying the blessings of sumptuous banquets at Abraham's side. The permanency of the reversal is expressed in v. 26 when Abraham pronounces that the great chasm is unbridgeable.

Verses 27–28: The rich man's second request is that Lazarus be sent to warn his brothers, revealing his myopic concern for members of his own elite circle. The rich man is not asking that Lazarus be resuscitated or resurrected from the dead, but that he communicate a message to the living in the form of a vision or dream. Such messengers are known in Greek literature,[57] and there are some instances in the scriptural tradition as well. Most notable is King Saul's consultation of the dead prophet Samuel through the medium at Endor (1 Sam 28: 7–20).[58]

Verse 29: Abraham tersely denies his second request. He answers that his brothers have Moses and the prophets and that they should listen to

---

56. Malina, "Wealth and Poverty," 357.

57. The motif of the appearance of a dead person in a vision or a dream is very old and universal. Lehtipuu (*Afterlife Imagery*, 191) states: "Often the dead appear in order to ask the living to do something to improve their conditions in the hereafter or to warn or console the living or to reveal some important information." See for example Homer, *Illiad*, 23, where the ghost of Patroclus appears to Achilles after he has been killed in battle. Patroclus' ghost requests a proper burial since he is not allowed to enter Hades without one.

58. Hultgren, *Parables of Jesus*, 114. See also 2 Kgs 21:6 and Isa 8:19.

them. Abraham's reply is particularly stinging when we recognize that the rich man and his brothers are members of the urban elite class, the very social and religious elite charged with safeguarding and interpreting the sacred tradition and ensuring the welfare of the people. As rich patrons, they have failed in their responsibility to observe and practice the teachings of Moses and the prophets to provide for the poor among them.

Verse 30: The rich man objects, insisting that someone from the dead should go to his brothers (ἀλλ' ἐάν τις ἀπὸ νεκρῶν πορευθῇ πρὸς αὐτούς). The request is for a messenger from the dead in a dream or vision, not resuscitation or resurrection. At last, the rich man acknowledges the necessity of repentance in stating that his brothers will repent (μετανοήσουσιν)[59] at the witness of a messenger from the dead. It is too little too late.

Verse 31: There are certain discrepancies between vv. 30 and 31 that lead the critical reader to suspect Lucan redaction of this last verse of the parable. Verse 30 states "if someone from the dead goes (πορευθῇ) to them" whereas v. 31 states "if someone should rise (ἀναστῇ) from the dead." Similarly, v. 30 states "they will repent (μετανοήσουσιν)" whereas v. 31 states "neither will they be persuaded (πεισθήσονται)." Verse 31 evinces Lucan redaction which is intended to coincide with the themes of the resurrection of Jesus (ἀναστῇ) and the persuasion of the rich to repent (πεισθήσονται). Perhaps the original language of v. 31 read, "Abraham replied, 'If they will not listen to Moses and the prophets, then they will not *repent* even if someone *goes to them* from the dead.'"[60]

In the end, the third and final request of the rich man is denied and the enduring validity of Moses and the prophets is upheld as the criterion of judgment. The parable concludes on a note of warning to the unmerciful and unrepentant rich of society, who fail to extend mercy and to repent by positive and concrete actions to benefit the poor and needy in their midst as is required of them by Moses and the prophets. Because of their lack of mercy and repentance, the parable asserts that the rich will be tormented in Hades even as the poor and needy inherit the blessings of eternal life they had once been assured of receiving.

---

59. Fitzmyer (*According to Luke*, 237) notes that this word for repentance is used frequently in Luke, five times as a noun and nine times as a verb.

60. This probability of Lucan redaction is heightened when one considers Crossan's examination of the connections between the concluding section of the parable and Luke 24 (Crossan, *In Parables*, 66–68). While I disagree with his dismissing the authenticity of vv. 27–31, the thematic links with Luke 24 are somewhat compelling. Nonetheless, I suggest that Lucan redaction is confined to the instances referred to in v. 31.

The Parable of the Rich Man and Lazarus

Narrative Context

The parable of the Rich Man and Lazarus is contained within the Lucan Travel Narrative (9:51—19:46) and more specifically within the self-contained subunit of Luke 16 with the topics of God, wealth, and the Law providing the immediate narrative context for the parable. The structure of Luke 16 is as follows:

16:1–9	*Parable* of the Dishonest Steward
16:10–13	*Teaching* on Faithfulness to God/Correct Use of Wealth
16:14–15	Pharisees *ridicule* Jesus/Jesus *ridicules* Pharisees
16:16–18	*Teaching* on Faithfulness to God/Correct Law Observance
16:19–31	*Parable* of the Rich Man and Lazarus

Notably, Luke 16 begins with the parable of the Dishonest Steward and concludes with the parable of the Rich Man and Lazarus providing two instances of use of wealth.[61] Verses 10–13 contain a teaching on faithfulness to God with regard to the correct use of wealth while vv. 16–18 contain another teaching on faithfulness to God with regard to correct Law observance. The heart of this structure in Luke 16 reports the Pharisees' contempt for Jesus and Jesus' reproach of the Pharisees in vv. 14–15: "You justify yourselves in the sight of others, but God knows your hearts; for what is of human esteem is an abomination in the sight of God."

Luke 16 would seem to suggest two important points for interpreting our parable within its immediate narrative context. On the one hand, Luke slants the interpretation of the parable in the direction of the mutual exclusivity of God (the greater matter) and wealth (the lesser matter). Not only are the wealthy alienated from God in earthly life, but that alienation becomes permanent in the afterlife. On the other hand, Luke also slants the interpretation of the parable by emphasizing the faithfulness to God (the greater matter) and the correct observance of the Law (the lesser matter). The wealthy are not as righteous before the Law as is generally presumed; otherwise, they would fulfill their duties toward the poor as commanded

---

61. Ball ("Unjust Steward," 329–30) suggests that these two parables should be interpreted in comparison with and in contrast to one another: "Applying the 'rule of two,' in the story of the Rich Man and Lazarus, we find behavior the precise opposite of that of the steward. The rich man conspicuously does not use his wealth to win friends in low places." "Thus both parables, one negatively, one positively, point to the message of Luke 16:9: 'I tell you, make friends for yourselves with dishonest wealth, so that when it fails, you will be welcomed into eternal dwellings.'"

by Moses and the prophets. The implication, then, is that they *a fortiori* are not faithful to God.

Luke's narrative use of the parable furthers one of the primary assertions of his Gospel; namely, the necessity of repentance among the rich in the form of positive and concrete socio-economic action to benefit the poor and the needy. Furthermore, the parable subverts the presumed righteousness and exclusivity of the social and religious elite through its depiction of an eschatological reversal of fortunes whereby the character of the poor man is exalted to rest at Abraham's bosom and the character of the rich man is condemned to torment in Hades. Evidence for this employment of the parable may be observed in Luke's use of traditional material, material unique to his Gospel and the predominant attitude toward wealth and possessions in the wider gospel context.

In some of the traditional material he shares with Mark and Matthew, Luke intensifies the themes of wealth and poverty, underscoring the socio-economic discrepancy between the rich and the poor.[62] Fitzmyer observes that Luke not only preserves traditional sayings of Jesus regarding these themes, he also accentuates and colors those sayings in accord with his own social and theological agenda and the needs of his own community:

> Obviously, he is not satisfied with what he has seen of the Christian use of wealth in his ecclesial community and makes use of sayings of Jesus to correct attitudes within it. . . . The point here is that this attitude toward material wealth in the Lucan Gospel did not originate with Luke himself. There is no need to think that it is not rooted in the preaching of the historical Jesus. But for his own reasons Luke has chosen to accentuate it, and he sees it as an imperative need in the Christian community for which he writes.[63]

Luke also records several parables and accounts unique to his Gospel that further elucidate the contrast between the socio-economic classes and the need for repentance, for example, the parables of the Good Samaritan, the Rich Fool, the Dishonest Steward, and the account of Jesus and Zacchaeus (19:1–10).

A radical and antagonistic attitude predominates in the Gospel and it is here that Luke's agenda becomes more evident.[64] Three key passages

---

62. Compare, for example, the synoptic accounts of Jesus' encounter with the rich young man (Matt 19:16–22; Mark 10:17–22; Luke 18:18–23).

63. Fitzmyer, *According to Luke*, 247, 248.

64. Ibid., 249–50.

embody this unabashedly hostile attitude in which the unrepentant rich and powerful are brought low and condemned while the poor and powerless are raised up and granted salvation. Mary's Magnificat (Luke 1:46–55), echoing Hannah's psalm of praise and vindication (1 Sam 2:1–10), depicts a reversal of human values and fortunes as the direct intervention of God in history: "He [God] has shown might with his arm, dispersed the arrogant of mind and heart. He has thrown down rulers from their thrones but lifted up the lowly. The hungry he has filled with good things; the rich he has sent away empty" (Luke 1:51–53).

Similarly, Jesus' proclamation from Isaiah 61 during his appearance in the synagogue at Nazareth at the outset of his public ministry announces the arrival of the year of God's favor as salvation for the poor and serves as a kind of political platform for his ministry: "The Spirit of the Lord is upon me, because he has anointed me to bring glad tiding to the poor. He has sent me to proclaim liberty to captives and recovery of sight to the blind, to let the oppressed go free, and to proclaim a year acceptable to the Lord" (Luke 4:18–19).

Finally, while the beatitudes are addressed to the poor in both Matthew and Luke, Matthew's version can be understood in a more spiritual sense while there is no mistaking the stark socio-economic language of Luke's rendition:

Matthew

- Blessed are the *poor in spirit*, for theirs is the kingdom of heaven. (Matt 5:3)
- Blessed are they *who hunger and thirst for righteousness*, for they will be satisfied. (Matt 5:6)

Luke

- Blessed are you who are *poor*, for the kingdom of God is yours. (Luke 6:20)
- Blessed are you *who are now hungry*, for you will be satisfied. (Luke 6:21)

Moreover, the blessings in Luke are contrasted with a complementary set of curses against the rich and represent a literal reversal of the current social and economic state of affairs, reminiscent of Abraham's reply to the rich man's first request in our parable:

- But woe to you who are rich, for *you have received your consolation.* But woe to you who are filled now, for you will be hungry. (Luke 6:24–25)
- Abraham replied, "My child, remember that *you received what was good during your lifetime* while Lazarus likewise received what was bad; but now he is comforted here, whereas you are tormented." (Luke 16:25)

Remember that for Luke, the terms "rich" and "poor" are employed as literary and metaphorical terms that refer not only to the economic sphere of existence, although they certainly mean that, but also to classifications of characters and their response (or lack of response) to God in the person of Jesus and to humanity. For all intents and purposes, Luke concludes, "No servant can serve two masters. He will either hate one and love the other, or be devoted to one and despise the other. You cannot serve God and mammon" (Luke 16:13).

CONCLUSION

In this chapter, we have isolated a subset of seven parables in the Lucan Travel Narrative that I call φιλάργυροι parables since together they possess certain affinities in terms of their rhetorical strategy of persuading the rich to repentance: the parable of the Good Samaritan (10:30–35), the parable of the Rich Fool (12:16–20), the parable of the Great Banquet (14:16–24), the parable of the Prodigal Son (15:11–32), the parable of the Dishonest Steward (16:1–8), the parable of the Rich Man and Lazarus (16:19–31), and the parable of the Pharisee and the Tax Collector (18:10–14). Each of these parables exhibit all or most of the following affinities that characterize this subset: They (a) are addressed by Jesus to one or more rich characters in the Gospel narrative; (b) demonstrate the need for repentance in the form of almsgiving or other merciful practice; (c) provide graphic and sometimes extreme characterizations of rich and/or poor characters; (d) utilize a rhetorical structure of reversal that involves orientation, disorientation, and reorientation, and; (e) are special "L" parables that exhibit a less radical and less negative attitude toward wealth and the wealthy when compared with other material in the Gospel.

The contours of these φιλάργυροι parables may be further delimited by the following four shared parabolic dynamics which are narrative structures and strategies geared toward the persuasion of the rich for repentance: Φιλάργυροι parables (a) are fictional stories explicitly grounded in the social, political, economic, and cultural realities of human existence; (b) metaphorically propose to the imagination an alternate vision of reality associated with aspects of Jesus' proclamation of the kingdom of God; (c) challenge and subvert the established order by guiding the hearer/reader through a process of orientation, disorientation, and reorientation, and; (d) elicit new responses, value judgments, relationships, expectations, and attitudes adequate to the alternate kingdom of God vision of reality proposed.

Finally, I presented an original translation of the parable and discussed the limited number of significant textual variants that appear in the tradition, along with a brief preliminary exegetical presentation that served to articulate the threefold structure of orientation / disorientation / reorientation and to illustrate by concrete example how the four parabolic dynamics achieve their purpose of persuading the rich to repentance.

With this foundation in place, I am now able to proceed with a socio-narratological analysis of each of the seven φιλάργυροι parables in the Lucan Travel Narrative and selected works from Lucian of Samosata in chapter 3.

3

Socio-Narratological Analysis of Selected Lucan Travel Narrative Parables and Selected Works from Lucian of Samosata

IN CHAPTER 2, I first isolated a subset of seven φιλάργυροι parables from the Lucan Travel Narrative that evince a certain affinity with regard to their rhetorical strategy of persuading the rich to repentance. I then examined four shared parabolic dynamics—logical strategies and structures employed to move the reader from a vision of reality that is exclusive and elitist to a vision that is inclusive, egalitarian, and associated with Jesus' preaching of the kingdom of God—by which these parables achieve their purpose. Finally, I presented the text of the parable of the Rich Man and Lazarus, its structure, and some brief preliminary exegetical notes that illustrate how these parabolic dynamics operate within this specific parable. The result of my analysis in chapter 2 is the proper identification of the parable of the Rich Man and Lazarus as one of seven φιλάργυροι parables in the Lucan Travel Narrative that together argue for the necessity of repentance among the rich.

In this third chapter, I shall begin by summarizing the socio-narratological method as described by David B. Gowler in his monograph entitled *Host, Guest, Enemy & Friend: Portraits of the Pharisees in Luke and Acts*, a method composed of two movements: character analysis and analysis of operative cultural scripts—culturally conditioned patterns of perceiving and behaving. Thereafter, I shall employ the socio-narratological method in an examination of the subset of seven φιλάργυροι parables in the Lucan Travel Narrative in an effort to discern a coherent profile of rich characters portrayed therein and additionally analyze operative cultural scripts to discover any recurring and convergent social concerns. Finally, I shall employ the socio-narratological method in an examination of selected works from Lucian of Samosata, attempting to discern a coherent profile of rich characters and convergent social concerns. The objective of this third chapter, therefore, is to present a concise socio-narratological analysis of selected Lucan Travel Narrative parables and selected works from Lucian of Samosata in an endeavor to highlight in each a coherent profile of rich characters and convergent social concerns and to determine how these two sets of analyses may mutually inform one another, and ultimately, in chapter 4, how such analyses may inform the interpretation of the parable of the Rich Man and Lazarus.

SOCIO-NARRATOLOGICAL METHOD

In *Host, Guest, Enemy & Friend*, Gowler uses the socio-narratological method to present a detailed and systematic character analysis of the Pharisees in Luke and Acts, informed by cultural scripts, illuminating the role that the Pharisees perform as characters in the narrative. My goal in this chapter is similar, although I will concentrate my study on the characters of the rich and the role that they perform in selected Lucan Travel Narrative parables, comparing and contrasting that profile with the profile of the rich as characterized in selected works from Lucian of Samosata. Before doing so, I take a moment to summarize the socio-narratological method as Gowler presents it.

Gowler argues that any method of character analysis must be supplemented by knowledge of the cultural scripts inherent in the text, in acknowledgement of the symbiotic relationship between characterization in a narrative and that narrative's cultural context. As we have seen, he describes the goal of the socio-narratological approach in the following way:

> A socio-narratological approach seeks to integrate these two concerns [narrative analysis and cultural scripts] into a cohesive methodology, where a narrative-critical perspective of characterization is merged with a knowledge of the socio-cultural and literary patterns of communication in the first century and inherent in the text of Luke-Acts. In effect, not only *can* cultural contexts be

merged with character analysis, but, in order for character analysis to be done correctly, cultural scripts *must* be utilized.[1]

Step One: Character Analysis

The first step in the socio-narratological method is character analysis, which can consist of either techniques for classifying characters or models for evaluating characters. Techniques for classifying characters generally identify similarities in character portrayals with the objective of categorizing these into established types or groups, as espoused by various scholars. E. M. Forster classified characters as either "flat" (constructed around a single trait with little or no narrative development) or "round" (constructed around more than one trait with capacity for narrative development).[2] W. J. Harvey broadened Forster's dichotomy by observing that characters exist on a continuum of complexity. Harvey classified characters as "protagonists" (fully established characters who experience conflict and change), "background characters" (characters who function primarily as mechanisms of the plot), or "intermediate characters" (characters with elements from the other two categories).[3] Yosef Ewen further differentiated character analysis by locating characters along continua on each of three axes, according to their degree of complexity, narrative development, and penetration into the character's inner life.[4] Finally, Baruch Hochman provided an even more complex method for classifying characters along a scale of eight bipolar axes.[5] However, Gowler observes that all of these techniques for classifying characters are essentially reductionistic and thereby inadequate for describing how readers actually experience characters in narrative texts. Much more helpful are models for evaluating characters.

Relying heavily on the work of Shlomith Rimmon-Kenan,[6] Gowler presents a coherent model for evaluating characters in biblical texts that he

---

1. Gowler, *Host, Guest, Enemy and Friend*, 27 (author's emphases).
2. Forster, *Aspects of the Novel*, 67–78.
3. Harvey, *Character and the Novel*, 56–58.
4. Ewen, "Theory of Character," 1–2.
5. Hochman, *Character in Literature*, 89. Hochman's bipolar axes consist of: stylization/naturalism; coherence/incoherence; wholeness/fragmentariness; literalness/symbolism; complexity/simplicity; transparency/opacity; dynamism/staticism; closure/openness.
6. Rimmon-Kenan, *Narrative Fiction*.

utilizes in step one of his socio-narratological method. Two factors must be considered when evaluating characters in a narrative text: explicitness (the clarity of the message) and reliability (the trustworthiness of the speaker). The most explicit manner for character evaluation is through direct definition, that is, the overt naming or judgment of a character's traits in the narrative. The overt presentation of a character's traits, whether brief or extended, creates in the mind of the reader an explicit, authoritative, and static impression. However, not all direct definitions carry the same weight. Direct definitions vary on a scale of reliability from high to low depending upon the level of authority invested in the one supplying the definition.[7]

The most reliable source for character evaluation is an omniscient, reliable narrator whose judgments the reader should accept as undeniably true and trustworthy. Even so, the reliability of the narrator can also vary based upon such factors as the scope of his or her knowledge and involvement in the narrative. There are different types of narrators. Narrators can be extradiegetic or intradiegetic—absent from or present in the story; narrators may also be heterodiegetic or homodiegetic—nonparticipant or participant in the story.[8] Thus, the degree of the narrator's involvement in the story inversely affects the reliability of the direct definitions supplied.

> A covert extradiegetic narrator, especially when he is also heterodiegetic, is likely to be reliable. . . . However, when an extradiegetic narrator becomes more overt, his chances of being fully reliable are diminished, since his interpretations, judgements, generalizations are not always compatible with the norms of the implied author. Intradiegetic narrators, especially when they are also homodiegetic, are on the whole more fallible than extradiegetic ones, because they are also characters in the fictional world. As such, they are subject to limited knowledge, personal involvement, and problematic value-schemes, often giving rise to the possibility of unreliability.[9]

In the biblical text, then, the most explicit and reliable character definitions are those that are direct and proceed from an extradiegetic-heterodiegetic narrator, as is the case with the omniscient gospel narrator of Luke-Acts. Other reliable sources for direct definitions may proceed from characters such as Jesus, the voice from heaven, or angelic creatures

---

7. Gowler, *Host, Guest, Enemy and Friend*, 55–57. Rimmon-Kenan, *Narrative Fiction*, 60–61.

8. Rimmon-Kenan, *Narrative Fiction*, 94–96.

9. Ibid., 103.

that possess the correct ideological point of view as espoused by the implied author. Some other characters, such as prophets or disciples, may also provide highly reliable character evaluations when presented by the narrator as under the inspiration of the Holy Spirit. Still other characters have varying and decreasing degrees of reliability, depending upon such factors as scope of knowledge and agreement or disagreement with the narrator's ideological point of view. The least reliable sources for direct definitions would include figures such as the Pharisees, the crowds, and other opponents of Jesus.

> Direct definition is the most explicit form of characterization, but it needs to be evaluated upon a descending scale of reliability. Reliability is the measure of the extent to which a speaker can be trusted, and direct definition varies in importance with the level of authority inherent in the voice which is speaking. The narrator and characters all may have varying degrees of reliability and have to be evaluated according to their congruence with the statements of the more reliable voices.[10]

Less explicit are indirect presentations that display various qualities and traits of characters in the course of the narrative but allow the reader to make the appropriate inferences as to what extent such qualities and traits reflect a character's true identity. Indirect presentations may take the form of speech, actions, external appearance, environment, and analogy that are interwoven throughout the narrative in descending degrees of explicitness and reliability.[11]

First, indirect presentation of character through speech can indicate traits through the speech's content and style, and what one character reports about another may characterize not only the one spoken about but also the one who speaks. The content of inward speech reported by the narrator, as in the case of a soliloquy, rates highest on the scale of reliability, followed in varying degrees of reliability by the content of the speech of the characters themselves as measured against agreement with the ideological point of view of the implied author. The style of a character's speech further may indicate such information as origin, social class, and quality of relationship with other characters in the narrative.[12]

---

10. Gowler, *Host, Guest, Enemy and Friend*, 72.

11. Ibid., 61–62.

12. Rimmon-Kenan, *Narrative Fiction*, 63–64; Gowler, *Host, Guest, Enemy and Friend*, 62–63.

Second, indirect presentation of character through action may proffer character traits as well, especially if such actions are habitual and hence symptomatic of traits that are more stable or intrinsic to that character. Nonetheless, atypical, one-time actions may serve to highlight some more dynamic trait normally hidden from view but no less important for understanding a character. Attention to acts of commission, acts of omission, and contemplated actions may provide further insights, although actions in general are less reliable than speech for evaluating character.[13]

Third, and furthest down the hierarchy of explicitness and reliability, are traits that can be inferred from a character's external appearance, environment, and analogous relationships. External appearance can include the character's permanent physical characteristics (height, weight, bodily condition, and integrity), along with more accidental features such as movements, clothing, and gestures. Environment can include the character's physical surroundings (room, house, urban or rural locale) and human surroundings (family and social class). Finally, both direct and indirect characterizations may be reinforced by way of analogy that emphasizes the similarity or contrast between the two elements or characters compared. Such comparison may either be stated explicitly or implicitly and may take the form of analogous names, landscapes, or characters.[14]

> Indirect presentation does not overtly announce character traits, but displays or exemplifies those traits or qualities. The reader then has to make the appropriate inferences. Therefore both the reliability and the explicitness of the characterization may vary. The importance of these references also varies with the order of presentation (e.g., the primary effect), with the sheer number of reported incidents, or with any other technique the narrator chooses to utilize.[15]

Indirect presentation is the primary means of characterization in Luke-Acts. Even where direct definitions do occur, they are frequently supplemented by and corroborated with multiple indirect presentations.[16]

---

13. Rimmon-Kenan, *Narrative Fiction*, 61–63; Gowler, *Host, Guest, Enemy and Friend*, 63–64.

14. Rimmon-Kenan, *Narrative Fiction*, 65–70; Gowler, *Host, Guest, Enemy and Friend*, 65–75.

15. Gowler, *Host, Guest, Enemy and Friend*, 72.

16. Ibid., 181–82. See further Gowler, "Characterization in Luke," 54–62.

Step Two: Cultural Scripts

The socio-narratological method's second step is the observation of the cultural norms that reflect upon the characters and their presentation in the text. It is at this point that the relevant cultural scripts—culturally conditioned patterns of perceiving and behaving—are highlighted and integrated into the process of apprehending the narrative development of the characters in question. The social-science models of first-century Mediterranean society are indispensable in this regard, as they help illuminate operative values, social dynamics, and worldview such as honor-shame values, patron-client relations, perception of limited goods, purity-pollution boundaries, and kinship relations.[17] Social-science models make explicit the social values, cultural dynamics, and the worldview implicit in biblical texts to which modern readers might otherwise remain oblivious. Models attempt to provide a contextual framework for better understanding the social and cultural worldview of the text from within a first-century Mediterranean consciousness. Two such social-science models are particularly relevant in our examination of the φιλάργυροι parables from the Lucan Travel Narrative and the selected works from Lucian of Samosata: the honor-shame values model and the patron-client relations model.

Bruce J. Malina describes honor and shame as pivotal values of the first-century Mediterranean worldview:

> From a symbolic point of view, honor stands for a person's rightful place in society, a person's social standing. This honor position is marked off by boundaries consisting of power, gender status, and location on the social ladder. From a functionalist point of view, honor is the value of a person in his or her own eyes plus the value of that person in the eyes of his or her social group. Honor is a claim to worth along with the social acknowledgement of worth. The purpose of honor is to serve as a sort of social rating which entitles a person to interact in specific ways with his or her equals, superiors, and subordinates, according to the prescribed cultural cues of the society.[18]

Without social acknowledgement, one's claim of worth lacks merit and deserves ridicule. Shame, then, is a positive value that indicates proper sensitivity to maintaining one's own public honor reputation and behaving

---

17. Gowler, *Host, Guest, Enemy and Friend*, 15–26.
18. Malina, *New Testament World*, 54.

accordingly, while shamelessness is a negative value that demonstrates inability to maintain that reputation or unwillingness to behave accordingly.

A person's honor can be ascribed, that is, associated with the status of one's birth; or it can be acquired, achieved through positive social actions such as public acts of generosity or heroism. Honor, like all other goods, is a limited commodity and therefore must be jealously guarded against loss. Nearly every social interaction outside the family unit is a potential threat to one's honor. In this agonistic cultural context, words and deeds take on heightened significance especially among social equals where public interactions become challenge-riposte contests for maintaining, gaining, or losing honor. One's honor status entails three areas: power (the hierarchical ability to control others), gender (adherence to defined male/female roles), and religion (adherence to appropriate relationships within a fixed hierarchy of superiors and subordinates).[19]

When considering the role of honor-shame values in the selected works from the Gospel of Luke and from Lucian of Samosata under analysis in this study, attention should be paid to the measure of ascribed or acquired honor associated with the characters in the narrative, to whether or not characters act in accord with their honor status, and especially to any honor challenges between or among characters. Challenge-riposte contests are honor challenges that may offer privileged insight into pertinent social concerns highlighted in the narrative and may provide readers with a further degree of indirect character definition and therefore must be accorded extra importance.

Challenge-riposte contests generally consist of three phases: (a) an individual initiates an honor-challenge to a social equal in the form of a word and/or action that can be either positive or negative; (b) the honor-challenge must be perceived as such by the receiver and witnessed publicly, and; (c) the receiver reacts to the honor-challenge with positive rejection, acceptance, or negative refusal of the honor-challenge. First, an honor-challenge is an attempt to enter another's social space, either to gain some share in that space through a mutually beneficial arrangement or to dislodge another from that space. The honor-challenge may take the form of words and/or actions that are positive (praise, a gift, a request for help) or negative (a verbal insult or physical threat/violence). Second, the receiver must perceive the challenger's potential to publicly damage (or enhance) his honor status and the severity of the threat (or opportunity). Only social

---

19. Ibid., 28–62. These honor-shame values are applicable on a collective as well an individual basis. See also Malina and Neyrey, "Honor and Shame," 25–65.

equals in the status areas of power, gender, and religion are able to engage in challenge-riposte contests; thus, social inferiors do not possess sufficient honor to rebuff a superior's action any more than a social superior is engaged by an inferior's appeal or affront. Third, the receiver of the honor-challenge must respond carefully, gauging how the public witnesses may judge that response. The recipient may respond with positive rejection (scorn, disdain, or contempt), with acceptance (the issuance of a counter-challenge), or with a negative refusal (a non-response that results in dishonor for the recipient). Whatever response is chosen, the verdict passed by the public audience is either a grant of honor taken from the receiver and awarded to the successful challenger or a loss of honor by the challenger in favor of the successful recipient.[20]

Another social-science model that is particularly relevant in our examination of the φιλάργυροι parables from the Lucan Travel Narrative and the selected works from Lucian of Samosata is the patron-client relations model. Halvor Moxnes defines patronage in the following way:

> Patron-client relations are social relationships between individuals based on a strong element of inequality and difference in power. The basic structure of the relationship is an exchange of different and very unequal resources. A patron has social, economic, and political resources that are needed by the client. In return, a client can give expressions of loyalty and honor that are useful to the patron.[21]

Three characteristics of patron-client relations—power, exchange, and solidarity—serve to describe the social and economic dynamics of the patronage system. While inherently unequal in power, the patron-client relationship is mutually beneficial on several counts. Patrons have instrumental, economic, and political resources (food, money, material resources, influence) and can offer clients needed support and protection. Clients, in exchange, can offer intangible resources such as respect, reputation, and enduring loyalty and provide an outlet for public expressions of generosity that enhance the patron's honor. There is a strong element of solidarity in such patron-client relations, linked to the mutually beneficial exchange of needed resources and associated with maintaining personal honor and

---

20. Malina, *New Testament World*, 34–37. The flowchart on p. 37 is especially helpful for visually understanding how challenge-riposte contests proceed. See also Malina and Neyrey, "Honor and Shame," 29–32.

21. Moxnes, "Patron-Client Relations," 242.

obligations.²² When the social distance between patron and client is too great, a broker-patron functions as a mediator, allowing access to the resources of a much more powerful patron.²³

When considering the role of patron-client relations in the selected works from the Gospel of Luke and from Lucian of Samosata under analysis in this study, attention should be paid to identifying which characters function (or fail to function) as patrons, clients, and brokers in the narrative, to how limited instrumental, economic, and political resources are distributed among characters, and especially to the mode of exchange operative between and among characters in the narrative. Particularly illustrative for our purposes are the dynamics of reciprocity as it applies to the distribution of basic human necessities of food, clothing, and shelter.

Jerome H. Neyrey describes three types of reciprocity: generalized reciprocity, balanced reciprocity, and negative reciprocity. Generalized reciprocity refers to assistance, whether financial, material, or influential, that focuses immediately on the interests and needs of another party. While the expectation of returned assistance is always implied, it is left indefinite and open-ended. Some forms of generalized reciprocity include hospitality and gifts and are characteristic of the kind of assistance among family members and kin. Balanced reciprocity refers to interactions in which the interests and needs of both parties are addressed. The rendering of equivalent benefits is insured by keeping track of the quantity and quality of the goods and services exchanged. Balanced reciprocity governs relations among neighbors and in the marketplace. Negative reciprocity, however, refers to one party extracting something from another without any intention for reciprocation, essentially covering theft, robbery, and all forms of forced expropriation of another's goods and services. Such negative reciprocity would be practiced only on those perceived as outsiders, strangers, or enemies.²⁴

Undergirding both social-science models of honor-shame values and patron-client relations is the first-century Mediterranean worldview of limited goods, that is, the perception that literally all resources, be they natural resources (land, water, animals), economic resources (food, clothing, money), or social resources (honor, status, power) exist in a finite, limited quantity and that they are perpetually in a state of short supply. It is equally apparent in this worldview of limited goods that there is no way to increase

---

22. See Eisenstadt and Roniger, *Patrons, Clients and Friends*, 48–49.
23. Moxnes, "Patron-Client Relations," 248.
24. Neyrey, "Ceremonies," 371–73.

directly the overall quantity of available goods, meaning that resources can be divided and redivided, but never increased. Therefore, individuals and families can only improve their natural, economic, and social positions at the expense of others:[25]

> Any apparent relative improvement in someone's position with respect to any good in life is viewed as a threat to the entire community. Obviously, someone is being deprived and denied something that is theirs, whether they know it or not. And since there is often uncertainty as to who is losing—it may be me and my family—any significant improvement is perceived not simply as a threat to other individuals or families alone, but as a threat to all individuals and families within the community, be it village or city quarter.[26]

Community stability and harmony, then, depend upon individuals and families remaining within the existing social arrangements and maintaining their inherited social status. In this perspective of limited good, those who upset the *status quo* by accumulating natural, economic, and social resources negatively impacted the well-being and harmony of the community. Honorable persons avoided accumulating wealth; instead they utilized various mechanisms of reciprocity to circulate needed resources among others. Those who nevertheless did accumulate wealth were considered greedy and dishonorable people—the rich—who were shamelessly driven to increase their resources at the necessary expense of others. Honorable persons also successfully maintained their status inherited at birth. Those who failed to maintain their status due to circumstances such as disease, injury, or debt were also considered dishonorable people—the poor—who were the socially ill-fated of any rank.[27]

In the following two subsections, I shall apply the socio-narratological method just described to the φιλάργυροι parables in the Lucan Travel Narrative in an effort to discern a coherent profile of rich characters portrayed therein and to discover any recurring and convergent social concerns.

---

25. Malina, *New Testament World*, 94–96.
26. Ibid., 95.
27. Ibid., 103–7.

CHARACTER ANALYSIS OF THE RICH IN SELECTED LUCAN TRAVEL NARRATIVE PARABLES

Each of the φιλάργυροι parables, with the exception of the parable of the Rich Man and Lazarus that will be treated in depth in chapter 4, will be examined below with regard to character evaluation as the first step in the socio-narratological method. The purpose of this examination is to discern the existence of a coherent profile with regard to the rich characters that populate this subset of Lucan Travel Narrative parables overall. Jesus as the reliable extradiegetic-heterodiegetic narrator of each of these parables provides the most trustworthy information through direct definitions.[28] Direct definitions are, nonetheless, supplemented and corroborated by multiple indirect definitions in descending orders of explicitness. The task at the end of this section, then, is to assess how both direct and indirect definitions of rich characters within these parables point to one coherent profile.

As a reminder, it is important to keep in mind that for Luke the terms "rich" and "poor" do not refer exclusively to the sphere of economic existence. Rather, as Luke T. Johnson points out, they are employed as literary and metaphorical terms that refer to classifications of characters and their response or lack of response to God in the person of Jesus and to humanity:

> The use of the terms rich and poor in Luke's Gospel go beyond the designation of economic circumstances to express conditions of powerlessness and power, being outcast by [people] or accepted by [them]. The preaching of the Gospel to the poor and the proclamation of woes to the rich signify that by God's visitation in the Prophet Jesus, these conditions are reversed, that the outcast are called to salvation and the [ones] who enjoy present acceptance are to be rejected. In the working out of the narrative, the poor are to be found in those who respond to the prophet, particularly the sinners and tax-collectors. . . . [T]he rich are found in those who reject the prophet, the leaders and particularly the Pharisees and Scribes.[29]

---

28. According to the terminology of Rimmon-Kenan (*Narrative Fiction*, 94–96), an extradiegetic-heterodiegetic narrator is one that is both absent from the story and non-participant in the story, and thus must be considered as a highly reliable and trustworthy source of information.

29. Johnson, *Literary Function of Possessions*, 165–66.

The Good Samaritan (10:30–35)

Direct Definition

There is little direct definition of the characters in the parable of the Good Samaritan. Neither the three primary characters—the priest, the Levite, the Samaritan—nor the three secondary characters—the victim, the group of robbers, the innkeeper—are directly defined to any significant degree by Jesus, the reliable narrator of the parable. Nonetheless, some key information is conveyed with the mention of each of the three primary characters. The priest (ἱερεύς, 10:31) is a representative of official Judaism, intimately associated with the Temple and responsible for the cultic worship of YHWH. The Levite (Λευίτης, 10:32), also a representative of official Judaism, is associated with minor cultic services and rituals in the Temple, along with scribal activity and the interpretation of Scripture. As such, both the priest and the Levite were esteemed "persons of exemplary piety whose actions would be regarded as self-evidently righteous."[30] As members of the privileged social and religious elite, they were rich in the Lucan use of the term, if not also wealthy.[31] The Samaritan (Σαμαρίτης, 10:33), on the other hand, is a socio-religious outcast, a despised member an ethnically mixed race of Israelites and non-Israelites that for historical reasons differed sharply from Jews on matters of worship and Scripture.[32] The mention of the Samaritan character would have evoked strong visceral antipathy in a Jewish audience, compounded by the fact that he is portrayed as a rich traveling merchant.[33]

Up to this point in the Gospel narrative, the reader has been presented with the very positive portrayal of the priest Zechariah (and his wife Elizabeth), described by the reliable narrator as "righteous in the eyes of God, observing all the commandments and ordinances of the Lord blamelessly" (1:6). Gabriel, an angel of the Lord, appears to Zechariah in the Temple (1:10–20), who later prophesies under the influence of the Holy Spirit

---

30. Green, *Gospel of Luke*, 431.

31. Against Johnson (*Luke*, 173) who states that the priests and Levites were not among the wealthy aristocracy.

32. Samaritans occupied the territory between Judea and Galilee, worshiped YHWH on Mount Gerizim rather than on Mount Zion, and recognized only the Pentateuch. See Bock, *Luke*, 969.

33. "Indication of his being a trader is the fact that he possesses oil, wine and considerable funds. Many traders were wealthy, having grown rich at the expense of others. They were therefore considered thieves." Malina and Rohrbaugh, *Social Science Commentary*, 347.

(1:67–79) after the birth of his son John. The reader would also remember the negative report of a Samaritan village that would not receive Jesus because he was on a journey to Jerusalem (9:52–53).[34]

Indirect Definition

Each of the three primary characters in the parable is described in a more nuanced fashion by way of indirect definition, allowing the reader to make the appropriate inferences according to a descending scale of explicitness.

Speech

No speech is reported for either the priest or the Levite. The Samaritan addresses the innkeeper with instructions for the victim's care, along with a formal promise of reimbursement for additional expenses incurred: "Take care of him. If you spend more than what I have given you, I shall repay you on my way back" (ἐγὼ ἐν τῷ ἐπανέρχεσθαί με ἀποδώσω σοι, 10:35). The Samaritan's use of ἐγώ . . . με has an emphatic force, formally assuring the innkeeper that he promises full reimbursement.[35]

Action

All three primary characters are depicted as traveling the same road between Jerusalem and Jericho. Both the priest and the Levite respond in a similar manner when encountering the robbery victim; they both pass by on the opposite side of the road (ἰδὼν αὐτὸν ἀντιπαρῆλθεν . . . ἰδὼν ἀντιπαρῆλθεν). In contrast to their acts of omission[36] in 10:31–32, the Samaritan responds in 10:33 with compassion (ἰδὼν ἐσπλαγχνίσθη).[37] The

---

34. Later on, however, Jesus praises a Samaritan as the only one out of ten persons healed of leprosy to glorify God and return to thank Jesus (17:15–16).

35. Entering into such an open-ended monetary relationship with an innkeeper was risky given the negative image of inns in antiquity and the probability for extortion. See Oakman, "Was Jesus a Peasant?" 122–23.

36. Whether it is fear of ambush, a concern for maintaining ritual purity, or some other motive, the key point of the matter is that neither the priest nor the Levite does anything for the victim. See Green, *Gospel of Luke*, 430.

37. The same verb is used to describe Jesus' reaction to the widow of Nain in 7:13 and the prodigal son's father in 15:20.

narrator then gives a detailed description of the Samaritan's seven compassionate actions in the remainder of the parable: he approached the victim, bandaged his wounds, anointed the wounds with oil and wine, put him on his own animal, led him to an inn, cared for him overnight, and prepaid the innkeeper two denarii for additional expenses until his return (10:34–35).[38]

External Appearance, Environment, Analogous Relationships

No mention is made of the external appearance of the primary characters. The physical environment envisioned for the bulk of the action may be the Pass of Adummim (Josh 18:17), a notorious part of the route fraught with violence and danger; hence the Hebrew appellation referencing blood.[39] The negative portrayal of the rich priest and rich Levite as representatives of the privileged social and religious class is starkly contrasted with the positive portrayal of the rich Samaritan on the basis of intensive compassionate action and complete absence thereof:

> [T]he pity and kindness shown by a schismatic Samaritan to an unfortunate, mistreated human victim stands out vividly against the heartless, perhaps Law-inspired insouciance of two representatives of the official Jewish cult, who otherwise would have been expected by their roles and heritage to deal with the "purification" of physically afflicted persons.[40]

From the definition of the primary characters in this parable, one may infer, as Fitzmyer rightly does: "The priest and the levite were not lacking in their love of God—the dedication of their status attests to that; but their love of neighbor was put to the test and was found wanting, whereas the Samaritan's shone true."[41]

---

38. See Bock, *Luke*, 1032–33.

39. Fitzmyer (*According to Luke*, 886) describes the steep 3,270 foot descent on the Roman road from Jerusalem (2,500 feet above sea level) to Jericho (770 feet below sea level) over a distance of eighteen miles through desert and rocky land.

40. Ibid., 884.

41. Ibid., 884–85.

The Rich Fool (12:16–20)

Direct Definition

Jesus as the reliable narrator presents two characters in this parable.[42] The first is a rich man (ἀνθρώπου τινὸς πλουσίου, 12:16). That the rich man is a substantial landholder is intimated by the mention of ἡ χώρα in v. 16, denoting that the property envisioned is certainly not a mere subsistence plot or even a normally sized field but rather something on the scale of a ridiculously expansive estate. In Luke, the term appears elsewhere in exclusive reference to a sizeable geographic district or region (2:8; 3:1; 8:26; 15:13–15; 21:21)[43] and may be used here hyperbolically to exaggerate the outrageousness of the rich man's wealth. Up to this point in the Gospel narrative, the reader has been presented with negative descriptions of the fate of the rich, involving divinely sanctioned reversals of fortunes as in the Canticle of Mary (1:53) and in the Sermon on the Plain (6:24).

The other character is God (ὁ θεός, 12:20), who is endowed with absolute reliability in the narrative, despite his intradiegetic-homodiegetic[44] status. God rebukes the man by calling him a fool (ἄφρων),[45] a devastating verdict that the reader must unequivocally accept at face value as true and that recalls the severe rebuke that Jesus directed at the Pharisees in 11:40 for their extortion, wickedness, and failure to give alms.

Indirect Definition

SPEECH

Most of the parable consists of the rich man's soliloquy in 12:17–19:

---

42. A similar parable exists in *Gos. Thom.* 63.

43. The term ἡ χώρα is so used in Acts as well: 8:1; 10:39; 12:20; 13:49; 16:6; 18:23; 26:20; 27:27.

44. According to the terminology of Rimmon-Kenan (*Narrative Fiction*, 94–96), an intradiegetic-homodiegetic character is one that is both present in the story and participant in the story. Normally, information derived from such characters should be considered less reliable because of factors such as limited knowledge or self-interested motivations. This is not the case in this instance, of course.

45. An epithet rooted in biblical tradition against those who are godless and comport themselves without wisdom, especially regarding the vanity of accumulating wealth and the inevitability of death. See Job 31:24–28; Ps 14:1; 53:1; Eccl 2:1–11; Sir 11:18–19. See further Donald, "Semantic Field," 285–92.

> He asked himself (διελογίζετο ἐν ἑαυτῷ), "What shall I do, for I do not have space to store my harvest?" And he said, "This is what I shall do: I shall tear down my barns and build larger ones. There I shall store all my grain and other goods and I shall say to myself, 'Now as for you, you have so many good things stored up for many years, rest, eat, drink, be merry!'"

Characters depicted as engaged in internal deliberations in Luke employing forms of the verb διαλογίζομαι are frequently portrayed in a negative light, associated with the hostility of the scribes and Pharisees (5:21–22; 6:8) and even a murderous plot (20:14). Here, the rich man's plan is to amass and preserve the bountiful harvest as security against the future and insurance for a life of leisure. God's speech qualifies the man as a fool and derides the futility of his machinations given the imminence of his death.

ACTION

The actions of the rich man are presented as contemplated actions that are not actualized within the parable narrative itself. Nonetheless, his plan as outlined in his monologue is revelatory of his negative character. He is godless in failing to acknowledge the divine for his good fortune, instead relying on amassed wealth for security. He is self-absorbed in failing to give alms in consideration of the needs of his neighbors. He is hedonistic as exemplified by his congratulatory self-exhortation: "Rest, eat, drink, be merry (εὐφραίνου)!" (12:19).[46]

EXTERNAL APPEARANCE, ENVIRONMENT, ANALOGOUS RELATIONSHIPS

No information is provided with regard to the characters' external appearance or physical environment (beyond an agricultural setting), and no comparison or contrast is drawn to indicate an analogous relationship between the characters.

---

46. This refrain represents a proverbial expression of hedonism, the unbridled pursuit of pleasure divorced from the expectation of judgment in earthly life or in the afterlife, censured in scriptural (Sir 11:19; Isa 22:13; 1 Cor 15:32) and other ancient literature. The verb εὐφραίνω appears elsewhere in Luke, notably in two other φιλάργυροι parables (Luke 15:23, 24, 29, 32; 16:19).

The Great Banquet (14:16–24)

Direct Definition

Jesus as the reliable narrator presents four primary characters in this parable:[47] the banquet host and three of the originally invited guests. The banquet host is first introduced in a generic manner (ἄνθρωπός τις, 14:16) but further defined in vv. 21–23 as master (ὁ κύριος) and in v. 21 as householder (ὁ οἰκοδεσπότης). The three originally invited guests are not directly defined. The parable also presents a large cast of secondary characters (a servant, other originally invited guests, and two groups of replacement guests) who are ancillary to the narrative.

Indirect Definition

Speech

The banquet host is rich, a member of the wealthy elite possessing both the social status and economic resources to stage a sizable banquet for his wealthy peers. The elevated socio-economic status of the banquet host and of the originally invited guests, although not directly defined, can be inferred through their respective speech. The first guest excuses himself from attending the banquet by stating: "I have purchased a field (ἀγρὸν ἠγόρασα) and must go to examine it . . . " (14:18), implying that he may be a rich absentee landlord living in the city. Since the dominant industry in pre-industrial societies was agriculture, engaging 80 to 90 percent of the population, control of the land signified both political and economic power.[48] A second guest also excuses himself stating: "I have purchased five yoke of oxen (ζεύγη βοῶν ἠγόρασα πέντε) and am on my way to evaluate them . . . " (14:19), implying that he may be a rich oxen trader and likewise owner of a rather large estate outside the city. A third invitee more tersely refuses the banquet invitation claiming unspecified familial responsibilities

---

47. A similar parable exists in *Gos. Thom.* 64.

48. Oakman ("Ancient Economy," 35) observes: "Land . . . was the most precious commodity for the ancient elites; for them control or ownership of land implied honorable lineage and was the material basis for household (economic) security. Thus people in antiquity who acquired wealth through commerce or other means normally attempted to achieve respectability by investing in land. Ancient societies as a rule resisted placing a money value upon land precisely to protect the status of long-standing elite groups and to discourage newcomers from obtaining respectability."

resulting from his recent marriage: "I have just married a woman (γυναῖκα ἔγημα), and therefore I cannot come" (14:20). While this third excuse dealing with marriage may appear disjunctive in comparison to patently commercial interests of the previous two, the institution of marriage in the first-century Mediterranean world was bound up with strategies for seeking economic and social advantage. "Especially among the wealthy elite, primary among motives for marriage was the generation of legitimate sons as heirs to ensure that property remained in the family."[49]

The banquet host perceives a concerted punitive measure of disentitlement by his rich peers and angrily commands his servant to bring in the poor as replacement guests. His description of them as the poor, the crippled, the blind, and the lame conforms to the stereotyped quartet previously referred to in 14:12–13 and reinforces the reader's apprehension of the banquet host as a member of the wealthy urban elite.

Action

Most of the parable consists of dialogue, with minimal action described.

External Appearance, Environment, Analogous Relationships

The external appearance of the primary characters is not described. The banquet host's commands to invite replacement guests are not a random ingathering of people but rather a targeted outreach to occupants of specific physical environments. In the first command, the servant is sent out to the streets and alleys (14:21), those areas of the city where the poorest of the urban non-elite would gather in public squares and market areas (τὰς πλατείας) and the narrow lanes and alleyways (ῥύμας) where they lived. In the second command, the servant is sent out to the highways and hedgerows (τὰς ὁδοὺς καὶ φραγμοὺς, 14:23), those areas outside of the city where the utterly destitute and outcast resided. The strongest of contrasts is drawn between the original invitees as obscenely rich and the substitute invitees as

---

49. "Another motive, slightly lesser perhaps, was the attraction of a large dowry (wealth) to which came attached the added benefit of a manager of household chores (labor).... [I]t is fair to say that acquiring a wife in the first place was governed more by forces that regulated the flow of wealth than by noble fancies for friendship." Braun, *Feasting and Social Rhetoric*, 77.

tragically poor. The rich banquet host, therefore, is depicted as employing a strategy of retaliatory rejection against his urban elite peers in favor of a radical reorientation toward the urban non-elite and outcast that he once sought to exclude.

The Prodigal Son (15:11–32)

Direct Definition

Jesus as the reliable narrator presents three primary characters in this extended narrative parable: a man / father, his younger son, and his older son. There is no further direct definition of these three characters beyond their stated familial relationship of a wealthy landowner and his two sons. Secondary characters include a citizen of a foreign land, hired day laborers (μίσθιοι), and household servants (δοῦλοι).

Indirect Definition

Speech

The speech of each of the primary characters is indirectly revelatory of some noteworthy character traits. The younger son (ὁ νεώτερος) impudently demands his share of the inheritance, demonstrating a decided lack of respect and a blatant desire to sever all kinship ties with his father. Nonetheless, finding himself in a desperate situation of poverty and hunger later on in a foreign land suffering famine, the younger son soliloquizes:

> How many of my father's hired workers have more than enough food to eat, but here am I, dying from hunger. I shall get up and go to my father and I shall say to him, "Father, I have sinned against heaven and against you (πάτερ, ἥμαρτον εἰς τὸν οὐρανὸν καὶ ἐνώπιόν σου). I no longer deserve to be called your son; treat me as you would treat one of your hired workers." (15:17–19)

The content of the younger son's soliloquy as reported by the reliable narrator is sincere and to be accepted by the reader at face value.[50] He exhibits

---

50. "While the basis for the son's repentance is clearly his own situation of desperate need, and a desire to improve his lot, it is wrong-headed to question his sincerity or to detect continuing pride in his bid to become an independent employee." Nolland, *Luke*, 784. Against Bailey, *Poet and Peasant*, 173–79.

repentance not so much for his hubris in prematurely demanding his share of the inheritance and then squandering it through a life of dissipation, but principally for his sin of disobedience; that is, the severing of kinship ties with his father. He repents and seeks to restore those ties, albeit only tenuously as a hired worker and not as a son.[51]

The father's speech reflect his joyous acceptance of the younger son upon his return: "Take the fattened calf and slaughter it. Then let us celebrate with a feast (φαγόντες εὐφρανθῶμεν), because this son of mine was dead, and has come to life again (νεκρὸς ἦν καὶ ἀνέζησεν); he was lost, and has been found (ἦν ἀπολωλὼς καὶ εὑρέθη)" (15:23–24).[52]

In stark contrast, his older son (ὁ υἱὸς αὐτοῦ ὁ πρεσβύτερος) reacts with anger and refuses to enter the house and participate in the joyous celebration. His contemptuous speech reveals his unforgiving attitude toward his repentant brother, while at the same time proclaiming his own righteousness to his father. He angrily expresses his resentment at the appearance that righteousness and obedience receive no recognition while sin and disobedience are rewarded: "Look, all these years I served you and not once did I disobey your orders; yet you never gave me even a young goat to feast on with my friends. But when your son returns who swallowed up your property with prostitutes, for him you slaughter the fattened calf" (15:29–30). The older son's lack of kinship language introduces elements of familial alienation that heretofore had not been revealed; he omits the respectful address of "Father" and refers to his sibling as "your son." His description of his relationship to his father sounds more like the language of a slave than that of a son. If he had a celebration, he would prefer to do so with his friends rather than his family. A reversal has taken place. "Accepting his unworthiness to be counted as a son, the younger [son] had opted for the status of a day laborer; having severed his relationship as a son,

---

51. "Critical to the development of this parable is how this loss and recovery are signified in familial terms. A younger son acknowledges his father as Father, but acts toward him in ways that are out of character according to normal canons of familial behavior. This leads eventually to his attempt to reconstrue [sic] their relationship as one of master/hired hand—a definition at odds with his father's persistence in regarding him in filial terms. Accepting his status as son, he is reconciled to his father and restored as a member of the family." Green, *Gospel of Luke*, 579.

52. The father's joy at the return of the repentant younger son recalls the "joy in heaven" and the "rejoicing among the angels of God" over one sinner who repents in 15:7 and 15:10.

Socio-Narratological Analysis of Selected Lucan Travel Narrative Parables

he hoped to reestablish it as a hireling. Ironically, the elder son comports himself now not as a son but as a slave."[53]

Action

Upon seeing the younger son returning from afar, the father is filled with compassion (εἶδεν αὐτὸν ὁ πατὴρ αὐτοῦ καὶ ἐσπλαγχνίσθη, 15:20; cf. 7:13; 10:33) and proceeds to act with demonstrably compassionate actions: he runs to his son, embraces him, and kisses him (κατεφίλησεν, 15:20; cf. 7:38, 45 where Jesus forgives a sinful woman). Such a public display of affection does not accord with what one would expect in an honor-shame society, potentially exposing the father to ridicule, but the father's overwhelming joy supersedes protocol.[54] The father interrupts the younger son's rehearsed speech to command his servants to fetch the best robe, a ring, and sandals that his son might be fully reinvested as a son, not a day laborer. He further commands his servants to slaughter the fattened calf for a feast celebrating the finding of the lost son. The older son is instead filled with anger (ὠργίσθη) and refuses to enter the celebratory feast, even after the father goes out to plead with him.

External Appearance, Environment, Analogous Relationships

While the younger son's external appearance upon his return can be surmised only from his sojourn in a foreign land, malnourished and tending swine, his restoration to the status of a son is externally symbolized with his literal investment with the best robe, ring, and sandals. The setting for the bulk of the action is the father's estate, perhaps substantial landholdings near a village. The younger son's moral estrangement from his father is replicated by his physical sojourn in the far-off land (χώραν μακράν).

Several strong comparisons and contrasts are drawn in the parable among the three primary characters that help illuminate certain character traits of the others. The younger son is initially disobedient, then repentant, while the older son is initially obedient, then unforgiving. The father

---

53. Green, *Gospel of Luke*, 585. Even so, the father attempts to utilize kinship language with the elder son, addressing him as "my son" (v. 31) and referring to his sibling as "your brother" (v. 32).

54. Ibid., 583.

responds to the return of the younger son with compassion, while the older son responds with anger.

The Dishonest Steward (16:1–8)

Direct Definition

Jesus as the reliable narrator presents two primary characters in 16:1: a rich man (ἄνθρωπός τις ἦν πλούσιος) and his steward (ὁ οἰκονόμος). The rich man, further defined as master (ὁ κύριός) by both the steward and the narrator, is likely an absentee landowner.[55] Significantly, it is the narrator who directly identifies the steward as dishonest in 16:8 (τὸν οἰκονόμον τῆς ἀδικίας), validating the essence if not the substance of the original accusations against him and is a qualification that the reader must take at face value as being entirely reliable. In contrast, the figure of a faithful and prudent steward (ὁ πιστὸς οἰκονόμος ὁ φρόνιμος) appears earlier in the Gospel narrative at 12:42 as one put in charge of his master's servants and who distributes the food allowance at the proper time. Two secondary characters are also featured as representative of a presumably larger group of the rich man's debtors.

Indirect Definition

Speech

The rich man readily believes the hostile charges of property-squandering lodged anonymously against his steward, calling him to render a final account. The rich man's speech reveals that he is stern and intolerant, as he does not extend the steward an opportunity to defend himself before summarily dismissing him, apparently uninterested in the veracity or falsehood of the accusations (οὐ γὰρ δύνῃ ἔτι οἰκονομεῖν, 16:2).

In response to the crisis of his impending termination, the steward engages in a soliloquy. His interior speech, introduced with the question τί ποιήσω in 16:3, is indirectly revelatory of the sense of privilege and status to which he has become accustomed. Access to his master's wealth and the

---

55. The explicit identification of the character as a rich man links it with two other φιλάργυροι parables from the Lucan Travel Narrative—the rich fool of 12:16 and the rich man of 16:19.

ability to serve as his agent in financial transactions has made the steward for all practical intents and purposes a rich man. Given this sense of privilege and status, he is both physically unable to engage in hard manual labor (σκάπτειν οὐκ ἰσχύω) and psychologically unable to beg (ἐπαιτεῖν αἰσχύνομαι); both options are unacceptable.[56] The steward settles on a self-preserving course of action that he calculates will insure his future well-being by creating enough goodwill among his master's debtors that they would welcome him into their homes.

The narrator provides the master's reported speech commending the steward for acting prudently (φρονίμως ἐποίησεν) at the conclusion of the parable in 16:8. The commendation is not for the steward's dishonesty but for his business acumen in reacting creatively to the impending loss of his stewardship and so providing security for his future—a kind of honor among thieves.

Action

The steward proceeds to call in his master's debtors one by one, significantly reducing the amount of debt owed. The debt reductions authorized by the steward are binding given that he still retains his position, at least until he submits his final rendering of accounts to his master. His strategy is to utilize his master's wealth in order to win friends for himself among his master's debtors, albeit by perpetuating his dishonesty.[57]

The amount of debt mentioned is itself instructive as to the great wealth of all the characters in the parable. The first debtor owes one hundred measures of olive oil (ἑκατὸν βάτους ἐλαίου, 16:6), the equivalent yield from 150 olive trees of some 875 gallons of oil valued at one thousand denarii, or over three years' salary for the average day laborer. The second debtor owes one

---

56. Fitzmyer, *According to Luke*, 1100. Green (*Gospel of Luke*, 590) observes: "For [the steward], loss of position as manager entails a forfeiture of social status, with the consequence that, initially, the only options he can entertain are manual labor and begging (v. 3); these locate him prospectively among the 'unclean and degraded' or even 'expendable' of society. What is more, his imminent departure as manager signifies his loss of household attachment, hence his concomitant concern for a roof over his head (v. 4)."

57. The steward's actions have been understood in a variety of ways, including that the steward reduces the debt by the amount of his commission (so Fitzmyer, *According to Luke*, 1101) or by the amount of interest due (so Derrett, "Fresh Light," 198–219). However, the master's praise of the dishonest steward's actions in 16:8 would lead the reader to suspect something sinister rather than benevolent has taken place.

hundred measures of wheat (ἑκατὸν κόρους σίτου, 16:7), the equivalent yield from one hundred acres of some 1,100 bushels of grain valued at 2,500 denarii, or over eight years' salary for the average day laborer.[58] While there may not be mathematical certitude with regard to these figures, the important point is that the amounts mentioned are substantial, if not hyperbolic. The rich man must be outrageously rich with debtors such as these.

External Appearance, Environment, Analogous Relationships

The external appearance of the primary characters is not described, nor is there mention of the parable's physical environment. A weak comparison is drawn between the rich man and the steward, in that both appear obsessed with wealth and how best to use it for their own self-interest.

The Pharisee and the Tax Collector (18:10–14)

Direct Definition

Jesus as the reliable narrator presents two primary characters in this parable: a Pharisee (Φαρισαῖος) and a tax collector (τελώνης) in 18:10. While these two characters are not directly defined any further in the parable itself, readers will remember descriptions and traits attributed to them earlier on in the Gospel narrative. The Pharisees stand as representatives of the socio-religious elite that generally remain unrepentant and become increasingly hostile to Jesus' ministry. Among other things, Jesus denounces the Pharisees for their greed and evil (ἁρπαγῆς καὶ πονηρίας, 11:39), for neglecting justice and love for God (παρέρχεσθε τὴν κρίσιν καὶ τὴν ἀγάπην τοῦ θεοῦ, 11:42), and by insinuation for committing adultery (μοιχεύει, 16:15, 18). Jesus labels them fools (ἄφρονες, 11:40) and warns of their hypocrisy (ὑπόκρισις, 12:1). The tax collector, on the other hand, stands as a representative of the despised non-elite who nonetheless respond positively to John's call for repentance (3:12), are baptized in accordance with God's plan (7:29–30), and who draw near to hear Jesus (15:1).

---

58. Bock, *Luke*, 1330–32.

Socio-Narratological Analysis of Selected Lucan Travel Narrative Parables

Indirect Definition

SPEECH

The prayers of the Pharisee and the tax collector provide reliable insight into their respective characters. The words of the Pharisee's self-aggrandizing prayer reveals an elitist perspective that presumes superiority over the rest of humanity, whom he disparages as sinfully rapacious, unrighteous, and adulterous (ἅρπαγες ἄδικοί μοιχοί, 18:11). Interestingly enough, the self-righteous prayer reveals his hypocrisy as these are the very sinful behaviors and attitudes that Jesus condemns among the Pharisees earlier on in the narrative. In contrast, the tax collector utters a simple prayer for mercy, recognizing his own sinfulness: ὁ θεός, ἱλάσθητί μοι τῷ ἁμαρτωλῷ (18:13).

ACTION

The Pharisee stands in the temple to offer his prayer of thanksgiving, fully self-assured and confident. Never mind that the prayer is less about thanksgiving for anything God has done and more about congratulating himself before God for his own piety. While the Pharisee enthusiastically lauds his ability to fast and tithe beyond what was expected, he makes no mention of almsgiving for repentance. The tax collector stands far off, does not raise his eyes, and beats his breast in a gesture of repentance.

EXTERNAL APPEARANCE, ENVIRONMENT, ANALOGOUS RELATIONSHIPS

The external appearance of the primary characters is not described. The parable takes place in the temple, significant for its identification as a holy place of worship and prayer before God, but also for its legitimizing function of defining and perpetuating social boundaries among persons and objects with regard to purity and pollution. Finally, an extreme contrast is drawn between the characters of the Pharisee and the tax collector; the one portrayed as prideful and self-justified, the other as appropriately humble and justified by God.

A coherent profile of the rich has emerged as a result of the foregoing evaluation of the rich characters that populate the φιλάργυροι subset of the

Tormented in Hades

Lucan Travel Narrative parables as demonstrated by way of direct and indirect definitions, the contours of which are delineated below. Two general types of rich characters in the φιλάργυροι parables may be distinguished: the unrepentant rich and the repentant rich. Both types may appear in a single narrative.

The unrepentant rich are those who:

- may normally be regarded as observant members of official Judaism (the priest, the Levite; the Pharisee);
- fail to compassionately assist those in obvious and immediate need of food, shelter, clothing, and medical attention (the priest, the Levite);
- possess and amass large quantities of food, land, and other material resources that they horde to the detriment of others in need (the rich fool);
- may be regarded as godless, seeking and celebrating their security in material wealth (the rich fool);
- engage in exclusive banquets designed to enhance their social standing among their elite peers (the banquet host and his original guests);
- do not give alms but employ commercial transactions and strategies that increase their wealth (the banquet host and his original guests; the dishonest steward), and;
- exhibit self-righteous behaviors and attitudes before God and others with contempt for the non-observant and non-elite (the older son; the Pharisee).

The repentant rich are those who:

- may normally be regarded as non-observant Jews or non-Jews (the Samaritan; the tax collector);
- take compassionate concrete actions to assist those in obvious and immediate need of food, shelter, clothing, and medical attention (the Samaritan);
- engage in inclusive banquets designed to enhance their social standing among the non-elite (the banquet host and his replacement guests);
- employ almsgiving and other strategies that redistribute wealth to those in need (the banquet host and his replacement guests; the dishonest steward), and;

Socio-Narratological Analysis of Selected Lucan Travel Narrative Parables

- exhibit humble behaviors and attitudes appealing for forgiveness and mercy from God and others (the younger/prodigal son; the tax collector).

OPERATIVE CULTURAL SCRIPTS IN SELECTED LUCAN TRAVEL NARRATIVE PARABLES

The second step in this socio-narratological study of the φιλάργυροι parables from the Lucan Travel Narrative is the analysis of operative cultural scripts, that is, culturally conditioned patterns of perceiving and behaving. In this regard, social-science models of first-century Mediterranean society are indispensable for helping to make explicit the social values, cultural dynamics, and the worldview implicit in biblical texts to which modern readers might otherwise remain oblivious. Models attempt to provide a contextual framework for better understanding the social and cultural worldview of the text from within a first-century Mediterranean consciousness.

A number of models exist, as elaborated by social-science biblical scholars.[59] These include models for honor-shame values, patron-client relations, perception of limited goods, purity-pollution boundaries, and kinship relations. While two such social-science models, the honor-shame values model and the patron-client relations model, are particularly relevant in our examination of the φιλάργυροι parables, reference to other models will be made where appropriate. When considering the role of honor-shame values, attention will be paid to the measure of ascribed or acquired honor associated with the characters in the narrative, to whether or not characters act in accord with their honor status, and especially to any honor challenges between or among characters. Likewise, when considering the role of patron-client relations, attention will be paid to identifying which characters function (or fail to function) as patrons, clients, and brokers in the narrative, to how limited instrumental, economic, and political resources are distributed among characters, and especially to the mode of exchange operative between and among characters in the narrative. Particularly illustrative are the dynamics of reciprocity as it applies to the distribution of basic human necessities of food, clothing, and shelter.

The purpose of this examination is to discover any recurring and convergent social concerns that are highlighted by Jesus as the reliable

---

59. Notable among these are Bruce J. Malina, Jerome H. Neyrey, Richard L. Rohrbaugh, John H. Elliott, and Halvor Moxnes.

extradiegetic-heterodiegetic narrator of each of these parables and by the Lucan narrator through the placement of the parable within its immediate narrative framework.

The Good Samaritan (10:30–35)

Narrative Frame

The parable of the Good Samaritan is set within the narrative framework of a public challenge-riposte contest for honor between Jesus and a lawyer. The lawyer's first question is a negative honor challenge as indicated by the narrator's use of the verb ἐκπειράζω (cf. 4:12), a hostile challenge to Jesus' status as teacher and his authority to speak on matters of the Law. Jesus deflects the challenge by posing a counter-challenge that prompts the lawyer to cite Deut 6:5 on the love of God and Lev 19:18 on the love of neighbor. Jesus endorses the lawyer's appropriate response, exhorting the lawyer to put the Law into practice while successfully defending his own honor status as an authoritative teacher of the Law.

Recognizing his initial failure to dishonor Jesus, the lawyer posits a second negative honor challenge soliciting Jesus' interpretation of the law in Lev 19:18 regarding the ambiguous identification of a neighbor that one is legally bound to love. The narrator notes the lawyer's disingenuous motive with the observation that he wanted to justify himself, a phrase used later on by Jesus to excoriate the Pharisees regarding their duplicitous Law practice (16:15). Jesus responds with the parable and a counter-challenge that reframes the lawyer's question from one of social identity to one of needs-based mercy. The lawyer is forced to acknowledge publicly the correctness of Jesus' interpretation and is again exhorted to act with mercy as a neighbor toward those in need.[60] At the conclusion of this challenge-riposte exchange, Jesus successfully defends and increases his honor status as an authoritative teacher of the Law, to the necessary corresponding decrease of the lawyer's honor status.[61]

---

60. "This is an important reminder of the message of the Sermon on the Plain (6:17–49), that practices are manifestations of one's character and dispositions; in the language of the current passage, love of neighbor flows out of radical love of God." Green, *Gospel of Luke*, 426.

61. Later on, the animosity between Jesus and lawyers is heightened. Jesus denounces the lawyers for placing heavy burdens on people they do nothing to alleviate (11:46), for rejecting prophetic interpretation of the Law (11:47), and for taking away the key of knowledge facilitating access to God (11:52).

Socio-Narratological Analysis of Selected Lucan Travel Narrative Parables

Parable

In the parable itself, the characters of the priest and the Levite are figures with the highest honor ascription in Jewish society due to their birth into priestly families and their close association with the Temple. The Samaritan, in contrast, is an outcast.[62] The parable gives no motive for the priest's and the Levite's failure to aid the victim, or for that matter, any motive for the Samaritan's compassionate assistance. Recourse to exculpatory theories about corpses and ritual purity are unnecessary.[63] The salient point is that the Samaritan demonstrated concrete actions of compassion as required by the Law while the priest and the Levite did not. As such, "the parable of the compassionate Samaritan thus undermines the determination of status in the community of God's people on the basis of ascription, substituting in its place a concern with performance, the granting of status on the basis of one's actions."[64]

The priest and the Levite also fail as patrons in that they possess economic resources (food, clothing, shelter, money) which the victim desperately needs. These resources the Samaritan extends in acts of generalized reciprocity to alleviate the immediate needs of the victim. Such generalized reciprocity is characteristic of the kind of assistance practiced among family members and kin; while the expectation of return assistance may be implied, it is left indefinite and open-ended.

In short, the parable depicts the Samaritan as acquiring honor because of his proper Law observance through his loving compassionate actions benefiting the victim and as practicing the kind of economic relations taught by Jesus in his Sermon on the Plain:

---

62. The temple purity system was organized around the core value of God's holiness, establishing and legitimizing social identity and boundaries within Jewish society and over against non-Jews. Maps of persons defined hierarchical relationships that if maintained constituted purity and if violated constituted pollution. "In the Lucan narrative the temple gradually emerges as an institution whose managers, interests, and ideology stand diametrically opposed to the ministry of Jesus and his community." Elliott, "Temple Versus Household," 223. The present parable is an example of the Lucan Jesus' contention that the Temple and its personnel no longer serve their primary purpose of mediating God's holiness and mercy.

63. For example, see Bailey (*Middle Eastern Eyes*, 293) who suggests that the priest could incur ritual impurity if the victim happened to be dead. Bock, *Luke*, 1030–31 summarizes other such explanations but emphasizes the point that the parable itself attributes no such motives to either the priest or the Levite.

64. Green, *Gospel of Luke*, 431.

> For if you love those who love you, what credit is that to you? Even sinners love those who love them. And if you do good to those who do good to you, what credit is that to you? Even sinners do the same. If you lend money to those from whom you expect repayment, what credit [is] that to you? Even sinners lend to sinners, and get back the same amount. But rather, love your enemies and do good to them, and lend expecting nothing back; then your reward will be great and you will be children of the Most High, for he himself is kind to the ungrateful and the wicked. Be merciful (γίνεσθε οἰκτίρμονες), just as [also] your Father is merciful. (6:32–36)

The Rich Fool (12:16–20)

Narrative Frame

The parable of the Rich Fool is set within the narrative framework of a public request for Jesus' assistance from a man in the gathered crowd. The request to arbitrate an inheritance dispute between siblings is a positive honor challenge in that it acknowledges Jesus' status as an authoritative teacher and interpreter of the Law. The request for such legal assistance is not unusual. However, Jesus scornfully responds with a positive rejection of the request to act as a judge between two brothers fighting over possessions. Instead, Jesus takes the occasion to exhort the crowd to guard against all forms of greed (πάσης πλεονεξίας) and teaches that one's life does not consist in becoming rich with possessions but in becoming rich toward God.[65]

Parable

The rich man in the parable, characterized hyperbolically by Jesus as a substantial landholder of outrageous wealth, has a plentiful harvest. He does not engage in generalized reciprocity by freely sharing his abundance as one would with family members and kin. Nor does he engage in balanced reciprocity by exchanging his abundance for other goods and services as one would among neighbors or in the marketplace. Rather, the rich man engages in a form of negative reciprocity, extracting needed alimentary resources for his self-indulgent conspicuous consumption: "Rest, eat, drink, be merry

---

65. Given the perspective of a limited-goods society, greed and the accumulation of possessions are tantamount to stealing.

(εὐφραίνου, 12:19)!" He has failed to act as a patron toward those in need around him, to serve as a broker of God's abundant material blessings intended to preserve the life of others. The rich man's attempt to set himself up as his own patron by amassing outrageous quantities of material resources is an affront to God's honor, essentially disavowing God the Father's role as patron and requiring the immediate surrender of the rich man's life.

The Great Banquet (14:16–24)

Narrative Frame

The parable of the Great Banquet is introduced with Jesus dining at the home of a leading Pharisee (εἰς οἶκόν τινος τῶν ἀρχόντων [τῶν] Φαρισαίων, 14:1) and in the course of the dinner conversation exhorts his host on the proper guests to invite. According to conventional practice, banquets were occasions for the social elite to maintain or enhance their honor status among their rich elite peers over and against the poor non-elite in displays of conspicuous consumption. Invitations were issued to persons with whom one desired affiliation and from whom one anticipated a mutually beneficial return exchange of goods, services, and status through balanced reciprocity: friends, brothers, relatives, and wealthy neighbors. Jesus exhorts his host to practice instead generalized reciprocity with the non-elite (cf. 5:29), with those unable to offer a return exchange of goods, services, and status as represented by the stereotyped quartet of the poor, the crippled, the blind, and the lame.[66] Jesus assures the host that practicing such generalized reciprocity with the poor is a mark of righteousness that will be reciprocated by God at the resurrection of the righteous.

This pronouncement by Jesus prompts another dinner guest to spontaneously utter a pious blessing (14:15; cf. 11:27–28) that serves as a catalyst for the parable illustrating Jesus' indictment of such exclusivist behaviors and attitudes of the rich elite, their conspicuous consumption, and their presumption of righteousness.

Parable

The host in the parable of the Great Banquet is depicted by Jesus as a member of the wealthy elite class, issuing a positive honor challenge to his elite

---

66. See further Neyrey, "Ceremonies," 361–87.

peers through his banquet invitation. The elite status of both host and originally invited guests is evident from the description of the meal as a great banquet for many (δεῖπνον μέγα, καὶ ἐκάλεσεν πολλούς) and from the commercial preoccupations of the excuse-makers. Hosting such exclusive banquets of and for the wealthy elite in patterns of balanced reciprocity was a primary means for the preservation and enhancement of one's honor.

> [The invitation] signifies an action aimed to secure admiration and respect and thus status and reputation within the conservative social reference group of the wealthy elite. The invitation is a gesture of a desire for affiliation or to remain affiliated. It represents the Lukan host's striving to construct his social biography in terms of allegiance to a particular class of people, the urban elite. . . . [T]hese elites stood exclusively over against others in the social organization of the city. They wove the fabric of their exclusive "sociability" in balanced patterns of giving and going to dinners and drinking parties there to preserve or enhance (and occasionally damage!) their public personae. . . .[67]

Unexpectedly, the banquet host's positive honor challenge to his elite peers is unanimously rejected by them. No motive for the wholesale rejection of the host's quest for honor and affiliation is supplied beyond the apparent punitive measure of disentitlement, evidently orchestrated to damage the reputation and social standing of the host. Regardless of the validity of the excuses,[68] couched in the language of polite formality and dissimulation, the invited guests are characterized as obsessed with protecting their collective rich elite status and as unquenchably desiring to accumulate wealth.

Thus publicly rejected, the angry host is faced with a choice—do nothing and suffer dishonor, or else do something to extract a measure of restored honor through vengeance.[69] The host implements a wholly un-

---

67. Braun, *Feasting and Social Rhetoric*, 105.

68. Attempts have been made to demonstrate the validity of the excuses with appeals to exemptions from participation in war listed in Deut 20:5–7 and 24:5. See Derrett, *Law in the New Testament*, 126–55, and Ballard, "Reasons for Refusing," 341–50. However, the invitation is to attend a banquet, not fight a war. Suffice it to say that the excuses neither constitute allusions to exemption to war nor constitute valid and legitimate reasons for rejecting the host's invitation.

69. "To allow one's honor to be impugned, hence taken, is to leave one's honor in a state of *desecration*—out of place, unclean, impure—and this would leave a person socially dishonored and dishonorable. On the other hand, to attempt to restore one's honor, even if the attempt is unsuccessful, is to return one's honor to the state of the sacred, to

orthodox strategy. Rather than explore methods for attempting to regain his previous status and seek eventual reintegration into elite circles, the host retaliates by rejecting those who rejected him through the deliberate invitation of substitute guests from among the least honorable of the non-elite. Having once sought to enhance his honor, elite status, and wealth among his peers, the host now casts his lot with those he once sought to exclude. Far from a one-time generous offer of a banquet for the poor as an act of benefaction, the host turns the tables on the rich elite and publicly manifests his desire for permanent affiliation with the poor and marginalized through sharing table fellowship with them.

> What is remarkable is that anger leads not to reprisal but to behavior that departs dramatically from the social system of reciprocity and status preservation that has thus far been characteristic of the socially elite in the larger narrative unit of vv. 1–24. Indeed, this "lord" now seems to repudiate the need for approval from his peers; he certainly acts in a way that despises the social order in which he had previously demonstrated his deftness.[70]

The radical reorientation of the rich banquet host toward the dishonorable poor exemplifies the ministry and teaching of Jesus regarding generalized reciprocity (14:12–14) and the necessity of repentance in the form of concrete actions benefiting the poor and those in need (11:37–52; 19:1–10).

The Prodigal Son (15:11–32)

Narrative Frame

The parable of the Prodigal Son is the third in a series of three parables directed to the Pharisees and scribes who murmur against Jesus for his association and table fellowship with dishonorable sinners (καὶ διεγόγγυζον οἵ τε Φαρισαῖοι καὶ οἱ γραμματεῖς λέγοντες ὅτι οὗτος ἁμαρτωλοὺς προσδέχεται καὶ συνεσθίει αὐτοῖς, 15:2). Their public murmuring is a negative honor challenge questioning Jesus' comportment as a teacher of the Law, a Law he is expected to uphold.[71] While the Lucan Jesus is depicted

---

purify it or cleanse it, leaving one socially honored and honorable (hence a person of valor, of standing)." Malina, *New Testament World*, 41.

70. Green, *Gospel of Luke*, 561.

71. "By implication, we may understand that the Pharisees and legal experts are essentially calling into question Jesus' status, asserting that he has stepped outside all

as sharing table fellowship with Pharisees as his peers (7:36–50; 11:37–44; 14:1–7), he is also shockingly depicted as breaking convention in sharing such fellowship with sinners (5:29–32; 7:34; 19:5–7). Jesus' repeated and deliberate violations of the map of persons, according to which meals are properly shared with persons of like honor status, provoke Pharisaic ire.[72] At issue is the varied response to the teaching and ministry of Jesus; on the one hand, the presumed self-righteousness of the elite and their lack of repentance, on the other hand, the acknowledged unrighteousness of sinners and their demonstrated acts of repentance (cf. 7:29–30; 18:9–14).

The first two parables in the series assert that there is more divine joy over the repentance of one sinner than over those righteous in no need of repentance (15:7, 10), an assertion more dramatically depicted in the present parable (15:24, 32). In countering the negative honor challenge before him, Jesus narrates the parable of the Prodigal Son demonstrating in allegorical fashion that the justification for his ministry of compassion toward repentant sinners is one of divine necessity (εὐφρανθῆναι δὲ καὶ χαρῆναι ἔδει, 15:32; cf. 12:19). By way of counter-challenge, Jesus urges the religious elite to comport themselves accordingly.

Parable

Rather than the language of patron-client relations or that of honor-shame values, the allegorical parable of the Prodigal Son utilizes the language of family and kinship relations to illustrate the dynamics of repentance and reconciliation that Jesus espouses as narrator. The characters are readily discernible and are associated with characters in the wider Gospel narrative. The primary image for God in the Lucan Travel Narrative is that of Father (11:1–13; 12:22–34), depicted as one who does not fail to provide food and clothing for his children, and who readily forgives and encourages forgiveness. Initially, the impudent younger son dishonors his father by his sinful behavior while the diligent elder son honors his father by his obedient observance.

> Critical to the development of this parable is how this loss and recovery are signified in familial terms. A younger son acknowledges

legitimate prerogatives by sharing the table with social refuse. Similarly, Jesus' reply in vv. 3–32 can be read as his attempt to ground the legitimacy of his behavior in the divine economy." Green, *Gospel of Luke*, 571.

72. On meals and table fellowship, see Neyrey, "Ceremonies," 361–87.

> his father as Father, but acts toward him in ways that are out of character according to normal canons of familial behavior. This leads eventually to his attempt to reconstrue their relationship as one of master/hired hand—a definition at odds with his father's persistence in regarding him in filial terms. Accepting his status as son, he is reconciled to his father and restored as a member of the family. The elder son, having never left home, nevertheless regards himself as a slave to his father and refuses to recognize his father's younger son as his own brother. Again the father persists in acknowledging the elder as his son and in doing so invites him to embrace the lost-and-found one again as brother.[73]

The repentance of the sinful prodigal is met with compassion from the father who calls for a great household celebration but is met with self-righteous anger on the part of the elder son. The father urges the elder son to be reconciled and celebrate his brother's return, but the parable remains open-ended as to the elder son's ultimate response.

The parable is a thinly-veiled counter-challenge to the Pharisees and scribes in 15:2 to extend compassion toward the repentant sinners and receive them as brothers and sisters as Jesus does through his practice of table fellowship, something they have been reticent to do. Instead, Jesus' narration of the elder son's speech provides a caricature of the religious leaders' self-righteous attitude (15:29–30) and their unwillingness to set aside their elite exclusivity in favor of God the Father's compassionate will.

> Throughout all this teaching of the Lukan Jesus, the household serves as the most apposite sphere and symbol of social life for illustrating features of life under the reign of God. In this connection the institution of kinship and family based on consanguinity and affinity provides a model for a community of fictive kin united by the bonds of mercy, faith, and filial obedience. The boundaries of this symbolical family or household of God are expanded to include the marginalized, the outcasts, Samaritans, and Gentiles.[74]

---

73. Green, *Gospel of Luke*, 579.
74. Elliott, "Temple Versus Household," 227.

Tormented in Hades

The Dishonest Steward (16:1–8)

Narrative Frame

The parable of the Dishonest Steward follows immediately after the parable of the Prodigal Son, except that Jesus addresses this parable to his disciples as his teaching regarding the appropriate use of wealth through almsgiving (16:9). Jesus exhorts his disciples, as he had exhorted the Pharisees, that they will be blessed if they practice generalized reciprocity that will be repaid by God only at the resurrection of the just (cf. 14:13–14).

Parable

The character of the dishonest steward is confronted by his rich master for squandering his property, and consequently will be relieved of his position after he renders a final account. The brief interim before his termination allows the dishonest steward sufficient time to implement a plan that insures that he will be granted hospitality among his former master's debtors. Apparently the steward engaged in negative reciprocity toward the debtors that was tantamount to thievery, either at the behest of his rich master or through his own devices. In any case, the dishonest steward's plan is to use his master's wealth to his own advantage by creating good will among those he had been defrauding to secure hospitality for himself in the near future.

Jesus implicitly draws an analogy between the shrewd actions (φρονίμως ἐποίησεν, 16:8) of the dishonest steward and the shrewd actions he advocates for his disciples when it comes to the proper use of wealth. Wealthy disciples are challenged to demonstrate repentance and distribute the resources that they do possess in the brief interval remaining in this age to their own advantage. By creating good will among the poor through almsgiving as a form of generalized reciprocity, they will make friends for themselves who cannot repay them in this life, but who will welcome them into eternal dwellings in the age to come.

> Taken on its own, this form of "making friends" would create a patron-client relationship, with the poor now indebted to serve and honor those who had provided for them. Such an understanding is undercut, though, by Jesus' related insistence that giving be done freely, with no strings attached, without expectation of return. In this case, "almsgiving" has as its consequence genuine

social solidarity between rich and poor, who act toward each other as "equal friends."[75]

The Pharisee and the Tax Collector (18:10–14)

Narrative Frame

The parable of the Pharisee and the Tax Collector appears to be addressed to a mixed audience of Pharisees and disciples (17:20, 22) but generally to "those who were convinced of their own righteousness and despised everyone else" (18:9). Such self-righteousness deceives one into believing that it is possible to live honorably apart from the need for repentance before God while shunning others for their perceived dishonorable living. As we have seen, such self-righteousness leads to exclusivist attitudes and behaviors that are radically opposed to the compassionate and inclusive teaching ministry of Jesus.

Parable

The parable itself draws a sharp contrast between two characters that epitomized honor and dishonor. Pharisees were honored for their piety and their exacting interpretation of the Law, while tax collectors were dishonored for their hated profession. Nonetheless, in the Lucan narrative dishonorable tax collectors are portrayed as open to John the Baptist's preaching repentance (3:12) and draw near to hear Jesus and share table fellowship with him (5:27–32; 7:29, 34; 15:1–2). Honorable Pharisees are portrayed as increasingly antagonistic toward Jesus' teaching and ministry and in turn are excoriated by Jesus on numerous occasions for their greed and evil (11:39), for neglecting justice and love for God (11:42), and for committing adultery (16:15, 18). They are fools (11:40) and hypocrites (12:1).

In the parable, Jesus teaches that human efforts to achieve righteousness are futile. It is God who justifies and grants honor to those who comport themselves according to a perspective that demonstrates an attitude of humble repentance before God as Father.

> According to Luke, Jesus' reading of this parable treats these two men in a way that idealizes one quality in each: One claims

---

75. Green, *Gospel of Luke*, 594.

> superior status for himself by comparing himself with and separating himself from others; the other makes no claims to status at all, but acknowledges his position as a sinner who can take refuge only in the beneficence of God. Convinced of his own righteousness, dependent upon his own acts of piety one asks for and receives nothing from God. The other comes to God in humility and receives that for which he asks, compassion and restoration.[76]

The foregoing survey of the φιλάργυροι parables has highlighted several recurring and convergent social concerns highlighted by Jesus as the reliable narrator of these parables and by the Lucan narrator through the placement of the parable within its immediate narrative framework.

- The law regarding love of neighbor is reframed by Jesus from one of obligations delimited by social identity to one of obligations identified by needs-based mercy; concomitantly, honor status is determined no longer by ascription but by performance of mercy towards those in need (Good Samaritan).
- Greed and the accumulation of wealth by the rich are condemned as forms of negative reciprocity that extract limited resources from the poor who need them to live (Rich Fool).
- Table fellowship as a means of maintaining or enhancing honor status among the rich elite over and against the non-elite poor in displays of conspicuous consumption is likewise condemned; rather than such balanced reciprocity, readers are exhorted to practice generalized reciprocity that benefits the poorest of the poor (Great Banquet).
- The institution of family and kinship serves as the model for repentance and reconciliation among all children of God the Father, such that exclusivity and self-righteousness have no place (Prodigal Son).
- Wealthy disciples are called to demonstrate repentance through the practice of almsgiving benefiting the poor as acts of generalized reciprocity that will accrue to righteousness at the resurrection of the just (Dishonest Steward).
- Self-righteousness leads to exclusivist attitudes and behaviors that are radically opposed to the compassionate and inclusive teaching ministry of Jesus (Pharisee and Tax Collector).

---

76. Ibid., 649.

Socio-Narratological Analysis of Selected Lucan Travel Narrative Parables

CHARACTER ANALYSIS OF THE RICH AND OPERATIVE CULTURAL SCRIPTS IN SELECTED WORKS FROM LUCIAN OF SAMOSATA

Several works from the second-century Cynic philosopher Lucian of Samosata (d. 180 C.E.) provide valuable insight into other roughly contemporary examples of literary characterizations of the rich and operative cultural scripts highlighting convergent issues of social concern. These rhetorical texts addressed the topics of wealth and poverty, achieving their purposes by frequently providing a comparison (σύγκρισις) between extreme examples from contrasting groups, in this case the rich and the poor, along with further characterization (ἠθοποιία) achieved through dialogue. In the words of Ronald Hock who first suggested the concept, it is quite legitimate and indeed necessary to cast the comparative net wider to include literary texts from the contemporary Greco-Roman milieu in an effort to reconstruct further the social and intellectual background of the parable of the Rich Man and Lazarus. Lucian of Samosata's works *Cataplus* and *Gallus* are especially helpful in this endeavor.[77]

The purpose of this subsection is to briefly survey these two works of Lucian of Samosata in an effort to discern a coherent profile of rich characters and the convergent social concerns contained therein. This survey will be conducted utilizing the same socio-narratological methodology as for the φιλάργυροι parables of the Lucan Travel Narrative, albeit in abbreviated fashion.

The Downward Journey or the Tyrant

Lucian's *The Downward Journey or the Tyrant* (ΚΑΤΑΠΛΟΥΣ Η ΤΥΡΑΝΝΟΣ)[78] describes the transportation of a shipment of the recently deceased from the realm of the living in the world above to the realm of the dead in the world below, the realm of Hades. At the conclusion of the journey, there is a scene of judgment for two of the principal characters, the rich tyrant Megapenthes and the poor cobbler Micyllus, and a description of their respective fates in the afterlife. The work proceeds by way of clever dialogue among the principal characters, providing for abundant indirect

---

77. See Hock, "Lazarus and Micyllus," 447–63. For the text of the *Cataplus* and the *Gallus*, along with English translations, see Harmon, *Lucian*, 2.1–57; 2.171–239.

78. Harmon, *Lucian*, 2.1–57.

definition and insight into the characterization of the rich and issues of social commentary.

The Downward Journey or the Tyrant opens with Charon and the Fate Clotho impatiently awaiting Hermes, who is delayed in his deliverance of dead persons for the ferry crossing to Hades. The delay, it turns out, was due to a rich tyrant's nearly successful escape back to the world of the living, his pursuit and eventual recapture amid his wailing, desperate bargaining, and attempted bribery of Hermes for his release. Unsuccessful with Hermes, the tyrant Megapenthes engages in an extended dialogue with Clotho to negotiate his release rather than board the ferry, a dialogue that is revelatory of Megapenthes' character and actions during his lifetime. Megapenthes variously argues that he needs to finish constructing his house, to inform his wife where he buried his great treasure, to complete the town walls and docks, and even to accomplish great military conquests. Clotho is not swayed.

The dialogue confirms the perception that in a limited goods society, the rich are necessarily evil and can only become rich at the expense of others, and frequently through callously murderous means:

> *Megapenthes*: You are unjust, Clotho, to bestow my property on my worst enemies.
> *Clotho*: Why, did not it formerly belong to Cydimachus, and did not you take it over after killing him and slaughtering his children upon him while the breath was still in his body?
> *Megapenthes*: But it was mine now.[79]

Nor is the tyrant above attempting to bribe Clotho with outrageous amounts of gold, similarly obtained by murderous means:

> *Megapenthes*: If you let me run away, I promise to give you a thousand talents of coined gold today.
> *Clotho*: What, you ridiculous creature, have you gold and talents still on the brain?
> *Megapenthes*: And I'll give you also, if you wish, the two wine bowls that I got when I put Cleocritus to death; they are of refined gold and weigh a hundred talents each.[80]

Megapenthes is finally forced upon the ferry and unwillingly transported to Hades to face judgment before Rhadamanthus. The philosopher Cyniscus prosecutes Megapenthes for his evil deeds that are as plain to see as

---

79. Ibid., 2.19.
80. Ibid.

the marks upon the soul (στίγματα επὶ τῆς ψυχῆς) at death, and include murder, theft, sexual immorality (corroborated by his bed and lamp as witnesses), and pride:

> *Cyniscus*: . . . he not only put to death more than ten thousand people without a hearing but confiscated their properties in each case; and after he made himself extremely rich, he did not leave a single form of excess untried, but practiced every sort of savagery and high-handedness upon his miserable fellow-citizens, ravishing maids, corrupting boys, and running amuck in every way among his subjects. And for his superciliousness, his pride, and his haughtiness toward all he met you never could exact from him a fitting penalty.[81]

For his crimes, Megapenthes is sentenced not to oblivion but rather to be denied a drink from the River of Forgetfulness and so to be tormented by the memories of his evil deeds and his former life of luxury:

> *Rhadamanthus*: How can he be punished? Shall he be thrown into the River of Burning Fire or turned over to Cerberus?
> *Cyniscus*: No, no! If you like, I will suggest [to] you a punishment that is new and fits his crime.
> *Rhadamanthus*: Speak out; I shall be most grateful to you for it.
> *Cyniscus*: It is customary, I believe, for all the dead to drink the water of Lethe?
> *Rhadamanthus*: Certainly.
> *Cyniscus*: Then let this man be the only one not to drink it.
> *Rhadamanthus*: Why, pray?
> *Cyniscus*: He will pay a bitter penalty in that way, by remembering what he was and how much power he had in the upper world, and reviewing his life of luxury.
> *Rhadamanthus*: Good! Let sentence stand in that form, and let the fellow be taken off and put in fetters near Tantalus, to remember what he did in life.[82]

The Dream or the Rooster

Lucian's *The Dream or the Rooster* (ΟΝΕΙΡΟΣ Η ΑΛΕΚΤΡΥΩΝ)[83] describes an extended dialogue between the poor cobbler Micyllus and his

81. Ibid., 2. 51.
82. Ibid., 2. 55, 57.
83. Harmon, *Lucian*, 2.171–239.

Tormented in Hades

rooster, who is really the philosopher Pythagoras reincarnated. The work opens with Micyllus angry with the rooster for awakening him from a fanciful dream in which he had been invited to dine at the house of the rich man Eucrates. Micyllus dreamt of a luxurious dinner of many courses of great variety served by waiters on plates of silver and gold, accompanied by musicians and entertainers. Sometime later, the rich man dies childless and wills his great fortune to Micyllus, who revels in his newly-gained wealth, only to be awakened from his reverie by the rooster's crow. The rooster chastises Micyllus for his thirst for riches:

> *Rooster*: Are you such a lover of gold and of riches (οὕτω φιλόχρυσος εἶ καὶ φιλόπλουτος), Micyllus, and is owning quantities of gold the only thing in the world that you admire and consider blissful?[84]

To illustrate the vexations of the rich in their obsession with wealth, the rooster takes Micyllus on a night journey to visit surreptitiously the houses of several rich men, among them Simon who lies awake preoccupied with safeguarding his accumulated riches:

> *Simon*: Well, then, that seventy talents is quite safely buried under the bed and no one else knows of it; but as for the sixteen, I think Sosylus the groom saw me hiding them under the manger. . . . It's my money these fellows are squandering, worse luck! But my cups are not stored in a safe place, either, and there are so many! I'm afraid someone may burrow under the wall and steal them: many envy me and plot against me, and above all my neighbor Micyllus.

A bit later, sleepless Simon continues his obsessive paranoia:

> *Simon*: At any rate it is best to stay awake myself and keep watch. I'll get up from time to time and go all about the whole house. Who is that? I see you burglar . . . oh! no, you are only a pillar, it is all right. I'll dig up my gold and count it again, for fear I made a mistake yesterday. There, now, somebody made a noise: he's after me, of course. I am beleaguered and plotted against by all the world. Where is my sword? If I find anyone. . . . Let us bury the gold again.[85]

---

84. Ibid., 2.197.
85. Ibid., 2.233, 235.

Socio-Narratological Analysis of Selected Lucan Travel Narrative Parables

The forgoing presentation of rich characters in the selected works of Lucian of Samosata is helpful for illustrating the stereotypes about the rich that readers of the Lucan parables may possess: they are murderous thieves, adulterers, sexually immoral, and proud. This profile, along with many other narrative details, will serve to aid the extended exegetical analysis of the parable of the Rich Man and Lazarus according to the socio-narratological method in the next chapter.

CONCLUSION

In this third chapter, then, a coherent profile of rich characters in the φιλάργυροι parables emerged whereby the rich are defined as either unrepentant or repentant. On the one hand, unrepentant rich characters are described as those who: (a) are normally regarded as observant members of official Judaism; (b) fail to compassionately assist persons in obvious and immediate need of food, shelter, clothing, and medical attention; (c) possess and amass large quantities of food, land, and other material resources that they horde to the detriment of others in need; (d) may be regarded as godless, seeking and celebrating their security in material wealth; (e) engage in exclusive banquets designed to enhance their social standing among their elite peers; (f) do not give alms but employ commercial transactions and strategies that increase their wealth, and; (g) exhibit self-righteous behaviors and attitudes before God and others with contempt for the non-observant and non-elite.

On the other hand, repentant rich characters are described as those who: (a) are normally regarded as non-observant Jews or non-Jews; (b) take compassionate concrete actions to assist persons in obvious and immediate need of food, shelter, clothing, and medical attention; (c) engage in inclusive banquets designed to enhance their social standing among the non-elite; (d) employ almsgiving and other strategies that redistribute wealth to those in need, and; (e) exhibit humble behaviors and attitudes appealing for forgiveness and mercy from God and others.

Next, my analysis of the operative cultural scripts in the φιλάργυροι parables has highlighted several recurring and convergent social concerns emphasized by Jesus as the reliable narrator of these parables and by the Lucan narrator through the placement of the parable within its immediate narrative framework. These social concerns include: (a) Jesus' reframing of the law regarding love of neighbor from one of obligations delimited by social identity to one of obligations identified by needs-based mercy and, concomitantly, the reframing of honor status as determined no longer by ascription but by performance of mercy towards those in need; (b) the condemnation of greed and the accumulation of wealth by the rich as forms of negative reciprocity that extract limited resources from the poor who need them to live; (c) the condemnation of table fellowship as a means of maintaining or enhancing honor status among the rich elite over and against the non-elite poor in displays of conspicuous consumption through balanced reciprocity and, thus the exhortation to practice generalized reciprocity that benefits the poorest of the poor; (d) the advancement of the institution of family and kinship as the model for repentance and reconciliation among all children of God the Father, such that exclusivity and self-righteousness have no place; (e) an exhortation to wealthy disciples who are called to demonstrate repentance through the practice of almsgiving benefiting the poor as acts of generalized reciprocity that will accrue to righteousness at the resurrection of the just, and; (f) the assertion that self-righteousness leads to exclusivist attitudes and behaviors that are radically opposed to the compassionate and inclusive teaching ministry of Jesus.

Finally, my brief survey of selected works from Lucian of Samosata likewise yielded a coherent profile of rich characters and convergent social concerns. Rich characters are described in unequivocally negative terms as having accumulated their great wealth through outright theft and murder. Their obsession with wealth and the luxurious lifestyle fills them with pride and affords them the ability to engage in various hedonistic pursuits that include lavish dinner parties and unrestrained sexual immorality. The principal social concern expressed in these works is the extreme and apparently unbridgeable socio-economic divide between the rich and the poor. The poor are helpless before the tyranny of the rich who suffer no juridical consequences in their lifetime and behave as if they are exempt from judgment in the afterlife.

These profiles of unrepentant and repentant rich characters, along with the recurring and convergent social concerns, gleaned from the foregoing analysis of the φιλάργυροι parables and selected works of Lucian will inform the socio-narratological exegesis of the parable of the Rich Man and Lazarus in the following chapter.

4

Socio-Narratological Exegesis of the Parable of the Rich Man and Lazarus (Luke 16:19–31)

IN CHAPTER 3, I summarized the socio-narratological method as described by David B. Gowler in *Host, Guest, Enemy & Friend: Portraits of the Pharisees in Luke and Acts* as a method composed of two movements: character analysis and analysis of operative cultural scripts—culturally conditioned patterns of perceiving and behaving. My examination of the subset of φιλάργυροι parables in the Lucan Travel Narrative consisted of the ways in which parable characters are directly and indirectly defined by the narrator and other characters along a scale of varying degrees of explicitness and reliability. Additionally, I examined the parables' narrative frames and the parables themselves through the lens of those culturally conditioned patterns of perceiving and behaving that typify first-century Mediterranean society and articulated by social-science models, with particular attention to the honor-shame values model and the patron-client relations model. The result of this examination of φιλάργυροι parables is rather variegated profiles of both unrepentant and repentant characters, the former presented negatively and the latter positively, along with the highlighting of several recurring and convergent social concerns emphasized by Jesus as the reliable narrator of these parables and by the Lucan narrator through the placement of the parable within its immediate narrative framework.

My brief survey of selected works from Lucian of Samosata likewise yielded a coherent profile of rich characters and convergent social concerns. Rich characters are described in unequivocally negative terms as having accumulated their great wealth through outright theft and murder. The principal social concern expressed in these works is the extreme and apparently unbridgeable socio-economic divide between the rich and the poor.

The objective of the present chapter, then, is to perform a detailed socio-narratological exegesis of the parable of the Rich Man and Lazarus, integrating the insights gained in chapter 3 about the profile of rich characters and convergent social concerns from the brief analyses of the other φιλάργυροι parables and the selected works of Lucian.

PROLOGUE: IDENTIFICATION OF THE PHARISEES AS ΦΙΛΆΡΓΥΡΟΙ (LUKE 16:14–18)

The narrator's explicit identification of the Pharisees as φιλάργυροι has a direct bearing upon the interpretation of the parable of the Rich Man and Lazarus, given that vv. 14–18 serve as a kind of prologue to the parable highlighting the connections between love of money and honor on the one hand and false teaching and comportment on the other.[1]

Generally speaking, the love of money, or greed, appeared frequently in Hellenistic lists of vices. In Plato's *Republic*, for example, those who were desirous of money (*philargyroi*) or desirous of honor (*philotimoi*) are considered unfit for ruling the state.[2] This particular pairing of vices, however, appears in contemporary Hellenistic polemical contexts against false teachers. In the *Discourses* of Dio Chrysostom, for example, the double accusation is leveled against Cynic and Sophist philosophers as false teachers. The Cynics teach "with a view to their own profit and reputation, and not to improve you" (32.10) while the Sophists "won marvelous acclaim" and "amassed much wealth" in contrast to poor Socrates who "was not driven by his poverty to accept anything" (54.1–3). Interestingly enough, Dio relates that in the latter case there is a reversal of fortunes after death

---

1. There is no change of audience between vv. 14–18 and the parable in vv. 19–31; the parable simply begins and the audience addressed is clearly the Pharisees. Most scholars (*pace* Sanders, *Jews in Luke-Acts*, 202–3) assert some sort of connection, however weak, between these verses and the parable.

2. *Republic* 1.347.

such that while the Sophists received reputation and wealth in this life their words perished, while Socrates suffered poverty and lack of fame but his words endured. Dio presents himself as a true philosopher who teaches in a disinterested fashion: "I have come before you not to display my talents as a speaker, nor because I want money (*argyriou*) from you; or expect your praise (*epainon*)" (35.1).[3]

The idea that the true teacher eschews money and honor is evident in the NT as well. Paul argues for the veracity of his teaching by reminding his audience that he and his coworkers' efforts were solely for their spiritual welfare.

> But as we were judged worthy by God to be entrusted with the gospel, that is how we speak, not as trying to please human beings, but rather God, who judges our hearts. Nor, indeed, did we ever appear with flattering speech, as you know, or with a pretext for greed (οὔτε ἐν προφάσει πλεονεξίας)—God is witness—nor did we seek praise from human beings (οὔτε ζητοῦντες ἐξ ἀνθρώπων δόξαν), either from you or from others, although we were able to impose our weight as apostles of Christ. (1 Thess 2:4–7a)

The theme of love of money and honor is likewise featured prominently in the polemic against false teachers in the pastoral letters: "For the love of money is the root of all evils (ῥίζα γὰρ πάντων τῶν κακῶν ἐστιν ἡ φιλαργυρία), and some people in their desire for it have strayed from the faith and have pierced themselves with many pains" (1 Tim 6:10).[4]

All this resonates well with what we find happening between the Pharisees and Jesus in Luke 16. The immediate context of vv. 14–15 is presented as an explicit denunciation of the Pharisees as false teachers precisely because they are lovers of money (φιλάργυροι) and try to justify themselves before people (οἱ δικαιοῦντες ἑαυτοὺς ἐνώπιον τῶν ἀνθρώπων). By way of contrasting implication, Jesus is the true teacher who seeks neither riches nor honor for himself. Verses 16–18, then, do not appear out of place but are germane to the argument that Jesus is the true teacher whose commitment to the enduring validity of the Law and the prophets stands in radical contrast to flawed Pharisaic teaching and comportment.

---

3. Moxnes, *Economy of the Kingdom*, 6–7.
4. See further 1 Tim 6:2b–16; 2 Tim 2:14—3:17; Titus 1:7–11.

The Pharisees as οἱ φιλάργυροι and οἱ δικαιοῦντες ἑαυτούς (vv. 14–15)

Direct Definition

These verses contain two direct definitions of the Pharisees, both of which are noteworthy for their highest possible degree of explicitness and reliability, thus meriting the reader's complete confidence. In v. 14, the Lucan narrator makes an explicit and authoritative direct definition of the Pharisees by way of a narrative aside: οἱ Φαρισαῖοι φιλάργυροι ὑπάρχοντες.[5] In v. 15, Jesus makes another explicit and authoritative direct definition through his verbal condemnation of the Pharisees: ὑμεῖς ἐστε οἱ δικαιοῦντες ἑαυτοὺς ἐνώπιον τῶν ἀνθρώπων. Taken together in rapid-fire succession, the negative characterization of the Pharisees as lovers of money and as public self-justifiers made by the highest possible authorities in the narrative, is as devastating as it is complete.

These direct definitions by the narrator and Jesus bring together and confirm two other direct definitions made earlier in the narrative. In 7:29–30, a narrative aside asserts that the Pharisees and lawyers reject the purpose of God for themselves by not receiving John's baptism of repentance, and so they fail to justify God (ἐδικαίωσαν τὸν θεόν) as all the people and the tax collectors do. Later on in 11:39, Jesus excoriates the Pharisees for their outward appearance of purity but inward greed and wickedness (τὸ δὲ ἔσωθεν ὑμῶν γέμει ἁρπαγῆς καὶ πονηρίας).

Indirect Definition

Speech

The Pharisees do not speak in vv. 14–15. Jesus, however, does respond verbally to the Pharisees' contempt for his teaching by exposing their public display of self-justification as abhorrent before God. In v. 15a, Jesus reminds the Pharisees that while all their outward display may impress people, God knows the inward reality of their hearts and cannot be deceived. God's knowledge of the human heart has a strong OT resonance and introduces

---

5. Note the close connection between 16:9 where Jesus exhorts his disciples to make "friends" for themselves by means of unrighteous mammon (ἑαυτοῖς ποιήσατε φίλους ἐκ τοῦ μαμωνᾶ τῆς ἀδικίας) and 16:14 where the Pharisees are called "friends of money" (οἱ Φαρισαῖοι φιλάργυροι ὑπάρχοντες).

the element of judgment according to divine, not human, standards (cf. 1 Sam 16:7; 1 Kgs 8:39; 1 Chr 28:9; Ps 7:10; Prov 21:2; 24:12). The human heart is featured prominently throughout Luke, notably in reference to God's judgment against the arrogant (1:51) and in exhortation for good human conduct (6:45; 10:27; 12:34).[6] Significantly, the narrator presents Jesus himself as able to perceive the human heart (5:22; 9:47), lending the reader reliable insight into Jesus' own identity and divine status.

Verse 15b has a quasi-proverbial feel and may have existed independently as a generic assertion. In context, Jesus' intended referent is clearly the conduct of the Pharisees who love money and who justify themselves, conduct that is an abomination in God's sight (βδέλυγμα ἐνώπιον τοῦ θεοῦ). The emotionally laden term βδέλυγμα is used extensively in the LXX and, especially in Deuteronomy and Isaiah, connotes idolatrous worship that is viscerally revolting before God.[7] The object of the Pharisees' idolatrous worship here is money (16:13, 14).

Action

The Pharisees' murmuring against Jesus because of his table fellowship with tax collectors and sundry sinners in 15:2 escalates to their scoffing at all the things that Jesus had taught since then (ἤκουον δὲ ταῦτα πάντα ... ἐξεμυκτήριζον αὐτόν), but perhaps especially his teachings in the parable of the Dishonest Steward on wealth and the impossibility of serving both God and Mammon in 16:1–13. The verb used for scoffing (ἐκμυκτηρίζω) denotes a vigorous show of contempt indicated by a turning up of one's nose and perhaps accompanied by an audible snort of derision.[8] The Pharisees publicly and finally discount Jesus as a legitimate Teacher of the Law along with the totality of his teaching and person.

---

6. Compare 14:11 for divine judgment-as-reversal against those who exalt themselves.

7. See Deut 7:25; 12:31; 18:12; 27:15; 29:17; 32:16; Isa 2:8, 20; 17:8; 41:24; 44:19.

8. This verb is found in the NT only in Luke, here in 16:14 and in 23:35 where the rulers scoff at the crucified Jesus. It appears in the LXX of the righteous one scorned by the enemy, for example in Pss 21:8 and 34:16.

Tormented in Hades

EXTERNAL APPEARANCE, ENVIRONMENT, ANALOGOUS RELATIONSHIPS

There are no indicators of external appearance or analogous relationships. The environment as indicated by the narrative is a public forum that includes the Pharisees and scribes, Jesus and his disciples, and the tax collectors and sinners with whom Jesus has been sharing table fellowship since 15:1.

Cultural Scripts

HONOR-SHAME

Jesus has been engaged in an extended challenge-riposte contest for honor that began when the Pharisees and scribes initiated a negative honor challenge by murmuring about Jesus' table fellowship with tax collectors and sinners (15:1–2). Jesus responds to their negative honor challenge and their attempt to discredit him as a teacher with a counter-challenge of his own comprised of a series of three parables demonstrating divine joy over the repentance of the unrighteous versus the righteous who do not repent (15:3–32). Having successfully defended his table fellowship and honor, Jesus then turns to teach his disciples about the proper use of wealth by recounting the parable of the Dishonest Steward (16:1–9) and the dangers of unrighteous mammon (16:10–13), all this in the presence of the same Pharisees, scribes, tax collectors, and sinners.

Jesus' teaching on wealth is rightly perceived by the Pharisees as a negative challenge to their own honor and comportment as teachers. Instead of continuing to engage Jesus as they had done up until this point in the narrative, they display scorn and contempt for him with their scoffing (16:14), effectively and definitively rejecting Jesus' teaching and person once and for all.

> [Luke] has repeatedly *shown* the Pharisees to be persons whose concerns with the maintenance and advancement of social standing negate any impulses toward care for the poor. Now he *tells* his readers the same thing, summarizing in a single expression, "lovers of money," what he regards as the most essential and unrelenting description of the Pharisees. In ridiculing Jesus, the Pharisees attempt to marginalize him by publicly rejecting any claim he might make to divine authorization. They do this, according to the narrator, because they are lovers of money—that is, people who

neglect the poor for the sake of their own community status, false teachers who reject God's purpose for themselves. (cf. 7:29–30)[9]

The implication is that since the Pharisees' hearts are not oriented toward God's purposes, they are necessarily unreliable interpreters and teachers of his Law.

Purity/Pollution

The language of purity and pollution is present in v. 15 with the mention of the term βδέλυγμα. While the Pharisees publicly present themselves as righteous, that is, esteeming the core societal value of God's holiness as replicated in the Law,[10] at heart they are unrighteous esteeming what is abominable and idolatrous in God's sight. This recalls Jesus' scathing condemnation of the Pharisees for their outward appearance of purity but inward impurity because of their failure to observe the Law through their extortion and wickedness, their neglect of justice and the love of God, and even their conveying impurity to those who come in contact with them and their teaching (see 11:39–44).

The Enduring Validity of the Law (vv. 16–18)

Direct Definition

There is no direct definition of characters in these verses.

Indirect Definition

Speech

Jesus continues the speech he began in v. 15 condemning the Pharisees for their public self-justification and idolatrous worship of money. Jesus asserts the enduring validity of the Law through its correct teaching and

---

9. Green, *Gospel of Luke*, 601. (Author's italics.)

10. "The core value influences how things are classified and where they are located. It is the overarching rationale for behavior, the principal justification for the shape of the system. The core value, moreover, is replicated throughout the system, giving it direction, clarity, and consistency. Abstractly, what accords to this value and its structural expressions is 'pure'; what contravenes it in any way is 'polluted'" (Neyrey, "Symbolic Universe," 275).

observance with the advent of the kingdom of God evident in his ministry, in sharp contradistinction to the teaching and observance of the Pharisees. The issue is germane to the question at hand: who has demonstrated possession of authentic teaching authority with regard to the Law—the Pharisees or Jesus?

Luke's presentation of Jesus' argument is admittedly difficult to follow but its primary thrust is that the Pharisaic approach to the Law itself has become idolatrous and perverted. The Law as taught and practiced by the Pharisees has frustrated God's purpose of salvation and has instead become a tool utilized by the religious elite to marginalize and oppress the poor. Jesus' ministry of announcing good news to the poor (4:16–21; 7:18–23) and his apparent contravention of the Law throughout the narrative by association with sinners and the forgiveness of their sins evinces an approach that emphasizes mercy over judgment.

> As Luke has developed it, "kingdom of God" connotes a new world order where the marginalized are embraced in the redemptive purpose of God. Hence, its promulgation has as one of its primary effects the fact that "everyone is urged to enter it," and this is precisely the universalism to which the Pharisees have taken offense. Thus, for Luke it is not that the "law and the prophets" belong to an old, now-bygone era, but that the Scriptures of Israel must be understood in light of the manifestation of God's purpose within the ministry of Jesus.[11]

Moreover, Jesus criticizes the way in which the Pharisees have perverted the Law to their own advantage, such that they publicly masquerade as righteous while they privately engage in the very idolatrous and licentious behaviors of which they accuse others. The particular example in v. 18 linking divorce and remarriage to adultery is more stringent than indicated in Deut 24:1–4.[12] It may be postulated that Jesus' interpretation is an indirect condemnation of the Pharisees' perversion of the laws on divorce and remarriage to suit their own social and economic advantage. While perhaps correct in a legalistic sense, their practice deals unmercifully with former spouses and children who are treated as mere commodities in their quest for more wealth and honor and serves as a concrete example of how the Pharisees treat the poor with contempt.

---

11. Green, *Gospel of Luke*, 603.

12. Fitzmyer, *According to Luke*, 1119–24. Compare Matt 5:31–32; 19:8–9; Mark 10:11–12; 1 Cor 7:10–11.

> [I]dolatry, wealth, and divorce are collocated as manifestations of pseudo-righteousness. Taken together, they are the means by which the Pharisees have distanced themselves from the very law they thought to uphold. They seek to advocate and preserve the law's relevance, but they are unable to do so because they lack insight into God's design. The irony of Luke's portrayal of the Pharisees is underscored later in the narrative by the Pharisee at prayer in the temple (18:9–14). Thanking God that he is not like those who swindle, who are unjust, or who commit adultery, he uses the very categories that Jesus has used in his allegations against Pharisees (cf. 11:39; 16:15–18).[13]

The response to the question of who has demonstrated possession of authentic teaching authority with regard to the Law, then, is clearly Jesus who accomplishes God's purpose of salvation by facilitating access to the Holy through emphasizing mercy over judgment. Thus, Jesus is indirectly defined as the true teacher and the Pharisees as false teachers.

Action

No action is narrated in these verses.

External Appearance, Environment, Analogous Relationships

There are no indicators of external appearance. An implied analogous relationship is drawn between Jesus as the true teacher who upholds the Law and is congruent in his external practice and internal disposition with regard to love of God and neighbor, on the one hand, and the Pharisees who appear to uphold the Law but are incongruent in their external practice and internal disposition with regard to love of God and contempt of neighbor, on the other. The environment as indicated by the narrative is the continuation of a public forum that includes the Pharisees and scribes, Jesus and his disciples, and the tax collectors and sinners with whom Jesus has been sharing table fellowship since 15:1.

---

13. Green, *Gospel of Luke*, 604.

Tormented in Hades

Cultural Scripts

Patron-Client Relations

The Pharisees in Luke are portrayed as entrenched representatives of the social and religious elite class, who possess an exclusivist vision of holiness that is diametrically opposed to the radically inclusive vision of the kingdom of God preached by Jesus. In their role as religious elite, the Pharisees controlled one of the primary symbols of religion, the Law, and in that role ought to have served as brokers or mediators of the redemptive power contained therein. However, time and again the Pharisees fail in this regard and instead are presented as blocking access to holiness and salvation.[14]

Luke 16:14–18 serves as a prologue to the parable of the Rich Man and Lazarus, explicitly identifying the Pharisees as φιλάργυροι. In so doing, the Lucan narrator prepares the reader to make connections between the Pharisees of the narrative and the rich man of the parable. Various elements from the profile of unrepentant rich characters gleaned from the other φιλάργυροι parables are relevant for how the reader perceives the Pharisees in these verses: they are normally regarded as observant members of official Judaism; they are nonetheless godless, seeking and celebrating their security in material wealth, and they exhibit self-righteous behaviors and attitudes before God and others with contempt for the non-observant and non-elite. The primary social concern these verses share with the other φιλάργυροι parables is that self-righteousness leads to exclusivist attitudes and behaviors that are radically opposed to the compassionate and inclusive teaching ministry of Jesus.

ORIENTATION: EARTHLY LIFE

As we have seen in chapter 2, the dramatic representation of human experience within an established vision of reality constitutes the first shared parabolic dynamic among the φιλάργυροι parables; namely, that *parables are fictional stories explicitly grounded in the social, political, economic, and cultural realities of human existence.* The realistic point of departure demonstrates the ultimate seriousness of the parable's subject. The initial emphasis on the realities of human existence, on everydayness, is intended to illuminate precisely those underlying human realities that are frequently hidden

---

14. Moxnes, "Patron-Client Relations," 256.

Socio-Narratological Exegesis of the Parable of the Rich Man and Lazarus

from more critical evaluation because of social custom or consensus and thus more resistant to potential modification. The points of departure in each of the seven φιλάργυροι parables present plausible situations and characters that resonate with real world experience from the perspective of the poor. From this established vision of reality, the poor are victims of neglect, violence, destitution, and even utter destruction at the hands of the rich who are portrayed stereotypically as consumed with maintaining or increasing their own social status and wealth. The characters and their behaviors are initially plausible, albeit at times drawn hyperbolically to enhance and intensify their realism.[15] By so intensifying the focus on the realities of the established order, these parables prepare the reader to confront the possibility of an alternate vision of reality by way of dramatic contrast.

The parable of the Rich Man and Lazarus begins by first orienting the reader to the established social, political, economic, and cultural human realities by narrating the extreme contrast in the earthly lives of the two primary characters. Each character is defined directly and indirectly by Jesus, the reliable narrator of the parable, according to the following parallel structure:

Orientation: Earthly Life

Rich Man's Life (v. 19)

Poor Man's Life (vv. 20–21a)

Disjunctive note on wild dogs (v. 21b)

The point of departure is the direct definition of the characters as rich and poor, definitions that are not simple objective descriptors but are stereotypical terms encoded with socio-narratological content from the first-century Mediterranean worldview of limited goods and from their particular use within the Lucan narrative. Each character is further defined indirectly by their actions, external appearance, and environment, resulting in a decidedly hyperbolic depiction of human reality.

> 19 There was a rich man
> who was clothed in a purple robe and fine linen garments
> and who feasted sumptuously every day.
>
> 20 There was also a poor man named Lazarus
> who lay at his gate, was covered with sores,

15. Funk, *Language*, 161.

Tormented in Hades

21 and who yearned to be fed with whatever fell from the rich man's table;
moreover, dogs came and licked his sores.

Direct Definition

The first character of the parable is directly defined as πλούσιος in v. 19. This definition immediately marks the rich man as an unsympathetic character. From the perspective of a limited-goods society, the presumption is that a rich person, or that person's ancestors, must have taken from others who now have less. When the amassing of wealth becomes an end in itself, the person dedicated to such behavior must be evil since he or she deprives others from meeting their needs for human living. To state that the rich person is evil is axiomatic.[16] From the perspective of the Lucan Travel Narrative, moreover, the profile of the unrepentant rich and the convergent social concerns from the φιλάργυροι parables add texture and context to the description of the rich man by illustrating different facets of censured behaviors and attitudes. For example, the reader would recall that the unrepentant rich are those who fail to compassionately assist persons in obvious and immediate need of food, shelter, clothing, and medical attention and that a primary social concern is the condemnation of greed and the accumulation of wealth by the rich as forms of negative reciprocity that extract limited resources from the poor who need them to live.

The second character of the parable is directly defined as πτωχός in v. 20. From a limited-goods perspective, the poor are victims of the greedy rich who deprive them of the resources they need to survive either directly through theft and violence or indirectly through culpable negligence. Or else they are the socially ill-fated who are unable to maintain their inherited socio-economic status because of the negative circumstances that have befallen them.[17] Generally speaking, the term πτωχός in Luke is associated with persons in a variety of negative circumstances including physical disease or deprivation (hunger, blindness, deafness, the crippled, the lame, the dead) or social marginalization (captivity, oppression, hatred, insult, exclusion).[18] This particular poor man is named

---

16. Malina, *Social Gospel of Jesus*, 103–5.
17. Malina, *New Testament World*, 105–6.
18. See Luke 4:18 (cf. Isa 58:6–7); 6:20–22; 7:22; 14:13, 21.

Λάζαρος, a name that foreshadows the divine assistance that he will receive in the parable's second movement.¹⁹

Indirect Definition

Speech

There is no reported speech in these verses.

Action

The indirect definitions associated with both the rich and poor men further intensify the polarization between these two characters. The action of the rich man who "feasted sumptuously every day" stands in stark contrast to the poor man who "yearned to be fed." The word for the rich man's feasting (εὐφραίνω) is used twice in Luke, on both occasions in φιλάργυροι parables denoting singular occasions celebrating a particularly fortuitous event.²⁰ The adverb λαμπρῶς suggests an extravagantly opulent feast whose splendor derives in part from the literal shining brilliance of the plates and goblets of silver and gold upon which it is served.²¹ By way of hyperbolic exaggeration, the rich man is described as holding such singularly extravagant and labor-intensive feasts on a daily basis!

In contrast, the poor man's passive action of "yearning to be fed" is the result of extreme privation that recalls the hunger pangs of the prodigal son in 15:16. In the same way that the prodigal son was so desperately hungry that he yearned to be fed with the pods intended for the unclean swine, poor Lazarus yearned to be fed with whatever fell from the rich man's table and was destined to be eaten by unclean dogs. Most likely, this table refuse

---

19. Fitzmyer (*According to Luke*, 1131) explains that the name Λάζαρος is "a grecized, shortened form of Hebrew or Aramaic 'Elʿāzār, known from the OT (e.g., Exod 6:23, son of Aaron)" meaning "God has helped."

20. Luke 12:19; 15:23, 24, 29, 32.

21. Compare the "splendid feast" described in Lucian's *The Dream or the Rooster* 11 (ΟΝΕΙΡΟΣ Η ΑΛΕΚΤΡΥΩΝ) where poor Micyllus dreamt of a luxurious dinner of many courses of great variety served by waiters on plates of silver and gold to the accompaniment of musicians and entertainers. He is later accused of being a φιλόχρυσος and a φιλόπλουτος. Compare also the δεῖπνον μέγα of Luke 14:16.

consisted of pieces of bread used to cleanse fingers and thrown on the ground as garbage.[22]

External Appearance, Environment, Analogous Relationships

The clothing of these two characters further distinguishes them. The rich man's clothing consists of an outer purple robe of fine wool dyed with imported Phoenician purple and fine linen undergarments imported from Egypt, connoting exceedingly rich or even royal status.[23] The labor-intensive process required to produce and import such vestments contributes to the reader's apprehension of the man's excessive wealth.

> Wool was used to produce vestments that advertized the social status of those who wore them. The process by which wool was "fulled" in a basin with special clay in order to render the cloth brilliantly white was time-consuming and costly. Clothing colored with Tyrian purple dye was likewise a striking luxury. Though white garments indicated membership among the elite, they were regarded as modest when compared with clothing dyed purple. White garments underneath a purple robe—this was the sign of the highest opulence.[24]

The poor man's virtual nakedness, in contrast, can be surmised from his visibly being covered with sores (εἰλκωμένος) and perhaps indicates that he is regarded as suffering divine punishment for some unspecified transgression, this in addition to the impression that he is crippled and needs to be transported by others to the rich man's residence in order to beg (ἐβέβλητο πρὸς τὸν πυλῶνα).[25] There is more to the disjunctive and curious narrative

---

22. Jeremias, *Parables of Jesus*, 148.

23. Fitzmyer, *According to Luke*, 1130–31. See Judg 8:26 ("the purple garments worn by the kings of Midian"); Esth 8:15 ("clothed in a royal robe of violet and of white cotton, with a large crown of gold and a mantle of fine crimson linen"); Rev 18:11–17. Compare Lucian's *Cataplus* 16: "When he [the rich tyrant Megapenthes] was dead, not only did he cut an utterly ridiculous figure in my eyes on being stripped of his pomp, but I laughed at myself even more than at him because I had marveled at such a worthless creature, inferring his happiness from the savour of his kitchen and counting him lucky because of his purple derived from the blood of mussels in the Laconian Sea."

24. Green, *Gospel of Luke*, 605.

25. Lazarus' nakedness is shameful and marks him as an unclean outsider to be avoided (Moxnes, *Economy of the Kingdom*, 91). Compare the Gerasene demoniac in Luke 8:27 who wore no clothes and lived among the tombs. For being afflicted with sores as divine punishment, see Exod 9–11; Deut 28:35; Rev 16:2. That Lazarus is crippled, or

detail in v. 21 than initially meets the eye. The dogs are neither compassionate creatures nor do they provide comfort by licking the poor man's sores. Rather, they are unclean scavengers roaming the city streets "that detect and taste the 'fresh meat' that the sores on Lazarus would represent to them. They wait for his death."[26] The wild dogs foreshadow the imminence of the poor man's death that occurs in the next verse.

The environment for this poignant juxtaposition is the gate of the rich man's residence (τὸν πυλῶνα αὐτοῦ). The term connotes the large impressive gateways at the entrances of the estates, palaces, temples, or cities and only serves to underscore the extent of the rich man's wealth and social status.[27] Indeed, the impression given is that the rich man possesses a palatial estate surrounded by walls at whose outer gateway Lazarus is situated. Also significant is that gateways traditionally served as the locus for judgment, foreshadowing the divine verdict of the reversal of fortunes in the parable's second movement.

The extreme characterizations of the rich and poor men in vv. 19–21 proceed in parallel fashion, highlighting the extent of the polarization based on the social and economic markers of food, clothing, and environment. Taken together, the ostentatious display of feasting sumptuously, dressing royally, and living in a palatial mansion marks the rich man as an exceedingly wealthy and prominent member of the ruling urban elite, while in contrast desperate hunger, virtual nakedness, and homelessness mark Lazarus as an exceedingly poor member of the marginalized and outcast. Such extreme contrasts in characterization are a feature of contemporary Greco-Roman philosophical writings, specifically rhetorical and Cynic texts that addressed the topic of wealth and poverty. Such rhetorical texts achieved their purposes by frequently providing a comparison (σύγκρισις) between extreme examples from contrasting groups. Both Lucian's *Cataplus* and the Lucan parable contain such comparisons. The nameless rich

---

at least too weak with hunger to walk on his own to the rich man's gate is suggested by the use of the pluperfect passive ἐβέβλητο: "The term is used of people who are confined to bed through illness (cf. Matt 8:6, 14; 9:2; Rev 2:2[2]) and is likely to suggest here Lazarus' inability to choose freely where he will be. We are probably to understand that Lazarus is positioned at the gate to beg, and that he is to all intents and purposes stuck there, living rough in the open, more or less where he begs" (Nolland, *Luke*, 828).

26. Hultgren, *Parables of Jesus*, 112. See 1 Kgs 14:11; 16:4; 21:24 for examples of dogs consuming the bodies of the dead, in this case, the bodies of enemies.

27. BDAG 897. In Acts 10:17, the word πυλών is used of the seaside house of Simon the tanner in Joppa and in 12:13–14 of the apparently large house of Mary, the mother of John Mark. In Acts 14:13, it is used of the gates of the temple or the city of Lystra.

man in the parable and the rich tyrant Megapenthes in the *Cataplus* are extreme examples distinguished by their fine clothing and luxurious banquets, prominent indicators of their abundant wealth. Poor Lazarus in the parable and poor Micyllus in the *Cataplus*, on the contrary, suffer deprivation due to their lack of sufficient clothing and nourishment.

> *Micyllus*: Besides, my position is not like that of the rich; our lives are poles apart, as the saying goes. Take the tyrant [Megapenthes], considered fortunate his whole life long, feared and admired by everybody; when he came to leave all his gold and silver and clothing and horses and dinners and handsome favourites and beautiful women, no wonder he was distressed and took it hard to be dragged away from them.... But as for me, having nothing at stake in life, neither farm nor tenement nor gold nor gear nor reputation nor statues, of course I was in marching order.[28]

Likewise, the sarcastic lament by Micyllus at death depicts his life of deprivation:

> *Hermes*: Do cry, however, even if only a little, for custom's sake.
> *Micyllus*: Well, I'll lament, then, since you wish it, Hermes—Alas, my scraps of leather! Alas, my old shoes! Alackaday, my rotten sandals! Unlucky man that I am, never again will I go hungry from morning to night or wander about in winter barefooted and half-naked, with my teeth chattering for cold![29]

Cultural Scripts

Honor-Shame

From the perspective of a limited-goods society and from the perspective of the poor, the direct definition of the first character as πλούσιος indeed marks him as an unsympathetic, if not evil character. From the perspective of the rich elite, however, prosperity was a sign of the divine blessing promised in Deuteronomistic theology.[30] In the narrative world of the parable, the rich man's prosperity would signal to the reader the presumption of divine blessing and honor; conversely, the poor man's misery would signal

---

28. Harmon, *Lucian*, 2. 15.
29. Ibid., 2. 20.
30. See especially Deut 28.

Socio-Narratological Exegesis of the Parable of the Rich Man and Lazarus

the presumption of divine curse and dishonor. It is these perspectives on human reality and their divine legitimization that the parable will undermine in its second movement.

Patron-Client Relations

Recall that Moxnes defines patronage in the following way:

> Patron-client relations are social relationships between individuals based on a strong element of inequality and difference in power. The basic structure of the relationship is an exchange of different and very unequal resources. A patron has social, economic, and political resources that are needed by the client. In return, a client can give expressions of loyalty and honor that are useful to the patron.[31]

While inherently unequal, the patron-client relationship is mutually beneficial on several counts. Patrons have instrumental, economic, and political resources and can offer clients support and protection. Clients, in turn, can offer non-tangible resources such as solidarity and loyalty, and provide an outlet for public expressions of generosity that enhance the patron's honor. While the type of reciprocity practiced (generalized, balanced, or negative) is conditioned by the kind of relationship that exists between the parties involved, other factors dictate certain responsibilities and obligations connected with wealth and status. From those persons who are wealthy or who are of high status, generosity in the form of generalized reciprocity beyond one's own kinship group is expected.[32]

The rich man in the parable is shown to fail grievously in that he refused to recognize poor Lazarus as an actual or potential client in desperate need of his assistance and protection through the practice of generalized reciprocity. Instead, the rich man practices balanced reciprocity by sharing elaborate and exclusive table fellowship with his elite peers on a daily basis.

DISORIENTATION: DEATH

A second shared parabolic dynamic among the seven φιλάργυροι parables is that they *metaphorically propose to the imagination an alternate vision of reality associated with aspects of Jesus' proclamation of the kingdom of God*. The

---

31. Moxnes, "Patron-Client Relations," 242.
32. Moxnes, *Economy of the Kingdom*, 34–35.

metaphorical quality of these parables refers to the analogy drawn in narrative form between two different visions of reality, the actual established order and a potential alternate vision. These two distinct but not entirely dissimilar elements are juxtaposed in such a way as to spark the imagination with new insights into the actual situation described and to propose the inauguration of an alternate vision of reality that cannot be conveyed through normal discursive speech.[33] The effectiveness of parables as metaphors lies in their power to provoke imaginative shock and create new meanings. The interpretive grid of the established order, the objective facticity of the social world, is peeled back as it were, and a new interpretive grid is superimposed to reorder the realities and priorities of human existence. The element of shock lies in this subversive, even destructive, potential.[34]

The parable of the Rich Man and Lazarus in its second movement of disorientation creates within the reader this kind of imaginative shock by juxtaposing in narrative form two different visions of reality, the actual established order and a potential alternate vision. In the parable's first movement describing earthly life, the rich man is blessed with prosperity and the poor man is cursed with suffering in accordance with the Deuteronomistic theological perspective. Now in the parable's second movement, the near simultaneous deaths of the rich and poor man are narrated according to the same parallel structure as the description of their earthly lives, but in reverse order and in counterintuitive fashion.

Disorientation: Death

Poor Man's Death (v. 22a)

Rich Man's Death (v. 22b)

Disjunctive note on reversal (v. 23)

The disorientation is oxymoronic. The normally expected outcome regarding the respective fates of the rich man and poor man upon death are directly opposed to the established view of reality: in the afterlife, the allegedly cursed poor man is blessed and the presumably blessed rich man is cursed. The reversal is narrated in a succinct, matter-of-fact fashion.

22 The poor man died
and was carried away by the angels to Abraham's bosom;

---

33. Funk, *Language*, 136.
34. Ibid., 139.

> the rich man also died
> and was buried.
>
> 23 Tormented in Hades, he raised his eyes
> and saw Abraham from afar
> and Lazarus at his bosom.

Direct Definition

There is no direct definition of characters in these verses beyond the earlier identification of two primary characters, the one as πλούσιος and the other as πτωχός. The patriarch Abraham is referred to here by name but does not play an active role in these verses.

Indirect Definition

Speech

There is no reported speech in these verses.

Action

Both men die while engaged in the very activities that typified their earthly lives; the poor man dies yearning to be fed, while the rich man dies feasting sumptuously. Given his miserable condition of lying desperately hungry, diseased, and virtually naked at the rich man's gate, the poor man's death is not unexpected. Significantly, no mention is made of a proper burial for the poor man, an important narrative detail in that it continues the perceived curse against him. "In Jewish tradition, to be refused burial, to be left exposed as carrion for scavenger animals (like dogs, v. 21), was tantamount to bearing the curse of God."[35] While it might even be surmised that the wild dogs performed their gruesome function of consuming his body, more likely the poor man is rescued from such an ignominious fate by the angels who carried him away before this could occur.[36] This divine intervention

---

35. Green, *Gospel of Luke*, 607.

36. The narrative detail about the poor man being "carried away by angels" is curious in that such a belief does not occur in Jewish writings before the mid-second century. Fitzmyer, *According to Luke*, 1132. Hultgren (*Parables of Jesus*, 113) suggests the phrase

provides the reader with the first instance of imaginative shock since it contradicts the expected outcome for the poor in the established reality.

In contrast, the rich man dies while feasting sumptuously and is most likely buried with all the pomp and ceremony befitting his elite status and momentarily continues the perception of his blessedness. Even so, the rich man's burial begs the question about the lack of a similar divine intervention on his behalf, providing the reader a second instance of imaginative shock that will emerge with full force in the following verse.

External Appearance, Environment, Analogous Relationships

There is no mention of the characters' external appearance in these verses. The portrayal of Lazarus at Abraham's bosom after death (Λάζαρον ἐν τοῖς κόλποις αὐτοῦ) has many possible associations. It may be a development of the OT idea of sleeping with one's ancestors (e.g., 1 Kgs 1:21; 2:10; 11:21; 4 Macc 13:17), or the designation of a place of honor to the right of the host at a banquet (ἐν τῷ κόλπῳ τοῦ Ἰησοῦ—John 13:23), or an association of intimacy (ὁ 'ὢν εἰς τὸν κόλπον τοῦ πατρός—John 1:18).[37] The banquet association should be favored because of the poor man's former exclusion from such in earthly life. This is consistent with the theme of reversal, in which case the figurative tables have been turned on the rich man.

The rich man finds himself tormented in Hades (ἐν τῷ ᾅδη ἐπάρας τοὺς ὀφθαλμοὺς αὐτοῦ, ὑπάρχων ἐν βασάνοις) and sees Lazarus at Abraham's bosom. Elsewhere in Luke, Hades appears in the context of unwillingness to repent and judgment (Luke 10:13–15). The text appears to portray the rich man and Lazarus as both located in Hades, albeit segregated in different locations according to their preliminary individualized fates. As we have seen from our review in chapter 1, contemporary Greco-Roman afterlife imagery was quite fluid and inconsistent. Lehtipuu observes that while the parable portrays the rich man and Lazarus in their individualized final states, elsewhere Luke presents a final, collective eschatological consummation of the end of time. She cautions that scholars should resist the temptation to harmonize the apparent contradiction into a coherent

---

evokes "the taking of Enoch to heaven by God (Gen 5:24) and the taking of Elijah to heaven in a whirlwind (2 Kgs 2:11)." Alternately, it may be a euphemism to describe those left unburied and eaten by dogs, birds, or other wild animals.

37. Fitzmyer, *According to Luke*, 1132.

Socio-Narratological Exegesis of the Parable of the Rich Man and Lazarus

eschatological doctrine that Luke may or may not have possessed.[38] In any case, the impression given in the parable is that while the rich man is physically segregated from Lazarus and Abraham by some meaningful distance within Hades, each remains visible to and within shouting distance of the other. As in the Epistle of Enoch (*1 Enoch* 92–105) where the righteous and the unrighteous are depicted as existing in separate, intermediate states in Hades before the advent of the final judgment, the rich man suffers preliminary punishments while Lazarus enjoys a preliminary period of rest in Abraham's bosom.[39]

Cultural Scripts

Honor-Shame

The rich man, accustomed in his earthly life to wealth, power, and honor, correctly perceives that his situation upon death is unbefitting his elite status and high honor rating. The situation is aggravated when he sees poor Lazarus exceedingly honored beside the patriarch Abraham. In a limited-goods perspective, the positive grant of honor awarded to Lazarus represents an inverse and proportional loss of honor for the rich man. His consignment to a location physically distant from that of honor elicits his resentment.

> Resentment means the psychological state of feeling distressed and anxious because the expectations and demands of the ego are not acknowledged by the actual treatment a person receives at the hands of others. It is a sense of moral indignation at the perceived injustice in the behavior of others toward me—not in keeping with my power, gender status, and social role.[40]

The rich man resents the dishonor accorded him, and he seeks to restore his honor in the parable's third movement.

---

38. Lehtipuu, *Afterlife Imagery*, 302–3. For Lehtipuu, eschatological expectations as presented in the Gospel were not central concerns but rather were at the service of more practical issues such as exhortations to repentance and the right use of possessions.
39. Compare *1 Enoch* 22; 4 Ezra 7:74–101.
40. Malina, *New Testament World*, 40.

REORIENTATION: AFTERLIFE

A third shared parabolic dynamic among the seven φιλάργυροι parables is that they *challenge and subvert the established order by guiding the hearer/reader through a process of orientation, disorientation, and reorientation*. In the parable's first movement the reader is oriented to the established order of reality, more precisely to some familiar aspect of the social, political, economic, or cultural world of the reader. This orientation may focus the reader's attention upon the aspect in question by way of hyperbolic portrayal of central characters, but it is a generally plausible presentation. The juxtaposition of the rich man and poor Lazarus in the parable underscores their socio-economic disparity. In the parable's second movement, the reader is abruptly disoriented as the expected dynamics of the world of common experience break down, resulting in imaginative shock. The parable presents the reader with an alternate vision of reality where characters do not behave as they normally do and expected outcomes are unfulfilled. The unexpected reversal of fortunes experienced by the rich man and poor Lazarus is disturbing.

Now in the parable's third and final movement, the reader is reoriented to an alternate vision of reality. Objective reality is viewed from an alternate perspective, one associated with dimensions of Jesus' proclamation of the kingdom of God. The parable depicts characters that must conform to new criteria for value judgments and human relationships—such as criteria based upon compassionate concrete actions to assist persons in obvious and immediate need of food, shelter, clothing, and medical attention as prescribed in Moses and the prophets. The parable demonstrates that those who fail to conform to the new criteria in the alternate vision of reality are doomed to exclusion and condemnation.

In the parable of the Rich Man and Lazarus, the rich man struggles mightily against conforming to the alternate vision of reality since he benefitted from the previously established order, value judgments, and matrix of human relationships. The existential struggle is narrated in the form of an extended dialogue between the rich man and the patriarch Abraham.

Reorientation: Afterlife

Rich Man's first request (v. 24)

Abraham's first denial (vv. 25–26)

Rich Man's second request (vv. 27–28)

Abraham's second denial (v. 29)

Rich Man's third request (v. 30)

Abraham's third denial (v. 31)

The implied presumption in the third movement of the parable, then, is that the established reality is in some way defective and requires challenge and subversion in order to conform more closely to the divinely ordained order encapsulated by the symbol of the kingdom of God. Each request-denial exchange between the rich man and Abraham further demonstrates defective aspects in the rich man's character and the permanency of the new state of affairs in the afterlife.

> 24 He cried out, "Father Abraham, have mercy on me!
> Send Lazarus to dip the tip of his finger in water and cool my tongue, because I am tormented in these flames!"
>
> 25 Abraham replied, "My child,
> remember that you received good fortune in your lifetime
> while Lazarus received only misfortune in his;
> now he is comforted here
> while you are tormented.
>
> 26 Moreover, a great chasm is established between you and us,
> so that those who would want to cross over from here to you cannot do so,
> nor can anyone from there cross over to us."
>
> 27 So he said, "Then I beg you, Father,
> send him to my father's house,
>
> 28 for I have five brothers, that he may warn them,
> lest they also come to this place of torment!"
>
> 29 Abraham replied,
> "They have Moses and the prophets;
> let them listen to them."
>
> 30 So he said, "No, Father Abraham!
> Certainly if someone from the dead would go to them, they will repent!"
>
> 31 Abraham replied,
> "If they will not listen to Moses and the prophets,
> then they will not be persuaded even if someone rises from the dead."

Direct Definition

The rich man and Abraham address each other utilizing kinship terminology. By repeatedly addressing the patriarch as his father (vv. 24, 27, 30), the rich man reasserts his identity and privileged status as a child of Abraham. He expects Abraham's special consideration to extricate him from his negative circumstance. Abraham reciprocates by acknowledging that the rich man is indeed a descendent (v. 25) but insists that he is powerless to intervene even if he were so inclined.

Indirect Definition

Speech

These verses are composed entirely of the dialogue between the rich man and Abraham, divided into three request-denial interchanges. In the first interchange (vv. 24–26), the rich man cries out to Abraham for mercy, a cry that is both deliciously ironic and presumptuous.[41] It is ironic because the rich man failed to demonstrate even the least amount of mercy toward the desperately hungry poor man he saw and heard begging for mercy just outside the gates of his palatial estate while he was inside feasting sumptuously on a daily basis. It is presumptuous because the rich man grounds the validity of his appeal upon kinship with Abraham whom he calls father, a kinship that if taken seriously would have required the rich man to act compassionately toward Lazarus—something he did not do. The claim of kinship affiliation with Abraham means nothing without the corresponding acts of mercy toward the needy:

> Produce good fruits as evidence of your repentance; and do not begin to say to yourselves, "We have Abraham as our father," for I tell you, God can raise up children to Abraham from these stones. . . . And the crowds asked [John], "What then should we do?" He said to them in reply, "Whoever has two tunics should share with the person who has none. And whoever has food should do likewise." (Luke 3:8, 10)

---

41. Green, *Gospel of Luke*, 608. The rich man pleads for mercy from Abraham (2 Esd 7:106), invoking God's promise and his privileged status as a child of Abraham (Gen 12:1–3; Luke 1:73).

Socio-Narratological Exegesis of the Parable of the Rich Man and Lazarus

Abraham denies the rich man's first request on two counts. On the one hand, Abraham cites the stark eschatological reversal in the afterlife that awaits the unrepentant rich and the poor, the working out of divine justice for those who were not appropriately punished or rewarded in their earthly life (see Luke 1:50–55; 6:20–26). On the other hand, Abraham indicates the great chasm in Hades separating the unrepentant rich from the poor, a chasm that has been divinely established.[42]

In the second interchange (vv. 27–29), the rich man requests that Lazarus be sent to his father's house to warn his brothers, revealing his continued myopic concern for the members of his own elite circle (cf. Luke 14:12–14). The communication requested by the rich man is that of a warning message to the living in the form of a vision or dream. Such messengers are a common feature in Greek literature and there are even instances from the OT.[43] But Abraham denies the request, citing the enduring validity of the Law (Moses) and the prophets.[44] Once again, the rich man's request is dripping with irony in that he fails to recognize poor Lazarus as a fellow child of Abraham, a failure of the very repentance he wants Lazarus to facilitate for his brothers.

In the third interchange (vv. 30–31), the rich man insists to no avail. Finally, the rich man acknowledges the necessity of repentance in stating that his brothers will repent (μετανοήσουσιν)[45] at the witness of a messenger from the dead. It is too little too late.

> Lazarus is not permitted to return, nor are the wealthy man's brothers granted any warning from beyond the grave of the fate awaiting them. Abraham thus refuses to grant an apocalyptic revelation of the fate of the dead, insisting that the witness of Moses and the prophets should suffice. The wealthy man, accustomed to extra considerations, will not take No for an answer. Continuing to speak from his supposed position of privilege, the wealthy man insists that, for his family, more is needed, that a special envoy is required.[46]

---

42. Note the theological passive ἐστήρικται in v. 26.

43. Herzog, *Subversive Speech*, 114. See also 1 Sam 28:7–20; 2 Kgs 21:6; Isa 8:19.

44. See for example Deut 14:28–29; Isa 10:1–4: 58:5–7; Jer 7:5–6; Amos 8:4–6; Zech 7:9–10.

45. Fitzmyer (*According to Luke*, 237) notes that the word for repentance is used frequently in Luke, five times as a noun and nine times as a verb.

46. Green, *Gospel of Luke*, 609.

Tormented in Hades

In the end, the third and final request of the rich man is denied and the enduring validity of Moses and the prophets is upheld as the criterion of judgment. The parable concludes on a note of warning to the unmerciful and unrepentant rich of society, who fail to extend mercy and to repent by positive and concrete actions to benefit the poor and needy in their midst as is required of them by Moses and the prophets. Because of their lack of mercy and repentance, the parable asserts that the rich will be tormented in Hades even as the poor and needy inherit the blessings of eternal life they had once been assured of receiving.

Action

The contemplated action in the rich man's first request has less to do with physical thirst, although this is a standard torment in Hades, than mental anguish as demonstrated by the use of the verb which denotes mental anguish (ὀδυνῶμαι)[47] and Abraham's negative response indicating that he must remember the good fortune of his lifetime (μνήσθητι ὅτι ἀπέλαβες τὰ ἀγαθά σου ἐν τῇ ζωῇ σου).[48]

The other contemplated action involves sending Lazarus as a messenger to warn the rich man's kin about the reversal of fortunes in the afterlife and the necessity of repentance. This once again serves to illustrate the rich man's character of concern for his own elite circle and kin.

External Appearance, Environment, Analogous Relationships

There is no mention of the external appearance of characters in these verses. The postmortem dialogue between the rich man and Abraham takes place in Hades. A couple of geographical features in the abode of the dead are mentioned in the parable and are relevant for the indirect definitions of the rich and poor men. First, the water that the rich man requests to quench his thirst

---

47. This verb is used exclusively by Luke in the NT, in Luke 2:48 here in 16:24, 25 and in Acts 20:38 to describe intense anxiety, mental anguish, and sorrow (Fitzmyer, *According to Luke*, 443).

48. For thirst and torment in Hades in relation to comportment during earthly life, see 2 Esd 8:56–59: "For when they had the opportunity to choose, they despised the Most High, and were contemptuous of his Law, and abandoned his ways. Moreover, they have even trampled on his righteous ones, and said in their hearts that there is no God— though they knew well that they must die. For just as the things that I have predicted await you, so the thirst and torment that are prepared wait for them."

Socio-Narratological Exegesis of the Parable of the Rich Man and Lazarus

in v. 24 is the water from the River Lethe.[49] Although it is not explicitly identified as such, the dead are given a drink from this river of forgetfulness upon their arrival in Hades so as to forget all that they have left behind in earthly life. One of the standard torments in Hades is to be denied this drink and so to be racked with unbearable mental anguish of the earthly life and loves now lost. The rich man's anguish is compounded since he is doomed to remember his past life of luxury and opulence. Compare the torment assigned to the tyrant Megapenthes after his judgment in Hades:

> *Rhadamanthus*: Enough witnesses! Come, strip off your purple robe that we may see the number of your marks. Well, well! The fellow is all livid and crisscrossed; indeed, he is black and blue with marks. How can he be punished? Shall he be thrown into the River of Burning Fire or turned over to Cerberus?
> *Cyniscus*: No, no! If you like, I will suggest you a punishment that is new and fits his crime.
> *Rhadamanthus*: Speak out; I shall be most grateful to you for it.
> *Cyniscus*: It is customary, I believe, for all the dead to drink the water of Lethe?
> *Rhadamanthus*: Certainly.
> *Cyniscus*: Then let this man be the only one not to drink it.
> *Rhadamanthus*: Why, pray?
> *Cyniscus*: He will pay a bitter penalty in that way, by remembering what he was and how much power he had in the upper world, and reviewing his life of luxury.
> *Rhadamanthus*: Good! Let sentence stand in that form, and let the fellow be taken off and put in fetters near Tantalus, to remember what he did in life.[50]

This interpretation of the first request is further supported by the use of the verb denoting mental anguish (ὀδυνῶμαι) and Abraham's negative response indicating that he is doomed to remember the good fortune of his lifetime. The presumption is that Lazarus has drunk the water from the River Lethe and so has no remembrance of his past life of utter misery and is enjoying the blessings of sumptuous banquets at Abraham's side.

A second geographical feature in Hades that plays a prominent role in the parable is that of the great chasm. The permanency of the reversal

---

49. Harmon, *Lucian*, 2.28. Alternately, the dead drink water from the Spring of Oblivion in *De Luctu* (Harmon, *Lucian*, 4.5).

50. Harmon, *Lucian*, 2.28–29.

is expressed in v. 26 when Abraham pronounces that the great chasm is unbridgeable.[51]

Cultural Scripts

Honor-Shame

The rich man issues a series of three positive honor challenges to Abraham by requesting his assistance and addressing him as Father. Normally, Abraham would be honor-bound to assist the rich man, but these are not normal circumstances.

Patron-Client Relations

The rich man and his brothers are members of the urban elite class, the very social and religious elite charged with safeguarding and interpreting the sacred tradition and ensuring the welfare of the people. As rich patrons, they have failed in their responsibility to observe and practice the teachings of Moses and the prophets to provide for the poor among them. The unrepentant rich practice an insular form of balanced reciprocity that neglects their responsibility to practice almsgiving and other forms of generalized reciprocity that benefit those in need.

CONCLUSION

The foregoing socio-narratological exegesis demonstrates how the parable of the Rich Man and Lazarus is geared toward persuading the rich to repent. It belongs to the subset of seven φιλάργυροι parables that exhibits a less radical and less negative attitude toward wealth and the wealthy when compared with other material in the Gospel, allowing for the very real possibility that some of the rich can indeed be persuaded to repentance and Christian discipleship. These parables attempt to move the reader through a process of orientation, disorientation, and reorientation, from a vision of reality that is exclusive and elitist to a vision that is inclusive, egalitarian, and associated with Jesus' preaching of the kingdom of God. In the case of the parable of the Rich Man and Lazarus, however, it demonstrates the ultimate consequences for the rich who nonetheless remain stubbornly unrepentant.

---

51. Compare *1 Enoch* 18:11–16; 21:1–10; 22:1–14.

Socio-Narratological Exegesis of the Parable of the Rich Man and Lazarus

In its first movement, the parable orients the reader to the established social, political, economic, and cultural realities of human existence with the juxtaposition of the rich man and poor Lazarus. In its second movement, the parable disorients the reader with imaginative shock by proposing an alternate vision of reality that depicts the characters' deaths and reversal of fortunes in Hades. In the parable's final movement, it reorients the reader to new criteria for value judgments and human relationship adequate to the alternate vision of reality in Jesus' proclamation of the kingdom of God. The parable of the Rich Man and Lazarus warns that the unrepentant rich, including the Pharisees and other φιλάργυροι in the Gospel narrative who fail to conform to these new criteria in the alternate vision of the kingdom of God, are doomed to exclusion and ultimate condemnation.

By way of conclusion, the next and final section will explore how the seven φιλάργυροι parables function together by utilizing this coherent rhetorical strategy of persuading the rich to repentance through the proper use of wealth and the establishment of proper social relations in Christian discipleship.

5

Conclusion: Rhetorical Strategy of Persuading the Rich to Repent in the Φιλάργυροι Parables of the Lucan Travel Narrative

SUMMARY

IN CHAPTER 1, I summarized modern research on the parable of the Rich Man and Lazarus in Luke 16:19–31 as it has developed since Jülicher precipitated the end of the allegorical method's dominance at the close of the nineteenth century. Generally speaking, scholarly interpretation of the parable has progressed in three different directions: the search for a parallel, the application of modern literary criticism, and the application of modern social-science criticism.

The search for a parallel to the parable of the Rich Man and Lazarus that occupied scholars through most of the twentieth century, while largely unsuccessful, cannot be called entirely unproductive. Gressmann's proposal for an Egyptian parallel drew attention to the validity of reading the parable over and against an extra-biblical text in order to gain insight into commonalities in narrative motifs such as the postmortem reversal

Conclusion: Rhetorical Strategy

of fortunes.¹ Hock's counterproposal for the Greco-Roman parallels in Lucian of Samosata's *Cataplus* and *Gallus* highlighted the commonality of the rhetorical presentation of extreme contrasting examples and further characterization through dialogue.² Nickelsburg's identification of resonances with Jewish apocalyptic in the Epistle of Enoch demonstrated the commonality of attitudes toward the rich and their possessions as well as further beliefs regarding postmortem imagery and justice.³ The current scholarly consensus summarized by Lehtipuu as the exploration of intertextual relations, common motifs, and images employed in the cultural milieu in the first-century Mediterranean world at once discounts and is indebted to the unsuccessful search for fixed parallels.⁴

Modern literary approaches to the parable have made several significant contributions to a better understanding of the Rich Man and Lazarus. Tannehill's description of Luke-Acts as a narrative unity places the parable within the greater controlling concept of God's plan for universal human salvation and humanity's continual rejection of God's plan. The parable illustrates in dramatic fashion the ultimate consequences for acceptance or rejection of the divine plan, and hence the necessity of repentance among the rich.⁵ Metzger's reading of the Travel Narrative presents an even more radical interpretation of the parable, one through which Jesus conveys an uncompromising, sectarian position that if the wealthy wish to participate in God's kingdom they must divest themselves of wealth so as to become poor.⁶ Finally, Lehtipuu demonstrated that since Luke's characterization of the rich and the poor are stereotypical representations of their respective groups, then any positive or negative evaluation of them is relevant to other rich and poor characters presented in the wider Lucan narrative as well as in the parable. The rhetorical effect of such characterization is to persuade the reader to share Luke's ideological point of view and system of values.⁷

Modern social approaches have made significant contributions to better understanding the parable of the Rich Man and Lazarus from within its

---

1. Gressmann, *Vom reichen Mann*.
2. Hock, "Lazarus and Micyllus."
3. Nickelsburg, "Riches, the Rich, and God's Judgment" and "Revisiting the Rich and Poor."
4. Lehtipuu, *Afterlife Imagery*.
5. Tannehill, *Narrative Unity*.
6. J. A. Metzger, *Consumption and Wealth*.
7. Lehtipuu, "Characterization and Persuasion."

appropriate social and cultural context. Bailey explores Gospel texts as they might be understood from an ancient Middle Eastern cultural perspective. His reading of the parable with attention to the cultural indicators of the rich man's behavior and speech reveals a character that is decidedly repulsive, one that is elitist, godless, and shamelessly manipulative of family ties.[8] Moxnes demonstrates how Luke condemns conspicuous consumption as practiced by the elite rich, and by extension the Pharisees, as creating and maintaining distinctions that effectively exclude others. Rather than practicing almsgiving and other redistributive mechanisms that represent morally good uses of wealth, the rich accumulate and protect surplus wealth and thus prevent the poor from fulfilling even their most basic needs for food, clothing, and shelter.[9] Finally, Malina's exposition on honor and shame as pivotal values of the first-century Mediterranean worldview allows the reader to appreciate that since honor is a limited commodity, Lazarus' postmortem increase in honor necessitates the rich man's decrease in honor. The rich man is revealed as utterly shameless in his argument with the patriarch Abraham.[10]

Despite these modern developments, a dialogue between the literary and social-science methods with regard to the parable of the Rich Man and Lazarus was still lacking. David B. Gowler's interdisciplinary socio-narratological method integrates the insights from both literary and cultural analyses of biblical narratives, an approach well-suited to a fresh understanding of the parable of the Rich Man and Lazarus from within its narrative and social contexts because it provides the crucial tools required to make explicit the often implicit dynamics of narrative character development and operative cultural scripts.[11]

In chapter 2, I isolated a subset of seven parables from the Lucan Travel Narrative that evince a certain affinity with regard to persuading the rich to repentance, examined four shared parabolic dynamics by which these parables achieve their rhetorical purpose, and presented some brief preliminary exegetical notes on the parable of the Rich Man and Lazarus by way of illustration.

This subset of φιλάργυροι parables that evince a certain affinity with regard to persuading the rich to repentance consists of the following narrative

---

8. Bailey, *Middle Eastern Eyes*.
9. Moxnes, *Economy of the Kingdom*.
10. Malina, *New Testament World*.
11. Gowler, *Host, Guest, Enemy and Friend*.

Conclusion: Rhetorical Strategy

parables: the parable of the Good Samaritan (10:30–35); the parable of the Rich Fool (12:16–20); the parable of the Great Banquet (14:16–24); the parable of the Prodigal Son (15:11–32); the parable of the Dishonest Steward (16:1–8); the parable of the Rich Man and Lazarus (16:19–31), and; the parable of the Pharisee and the Tax Collector (18:10–14). Each of these seven φιλάργυροι parables exhibit all or most of the following affinities that characterize this subset: They (a) are addressed by Jesus to one or more rich characters in the Gospel narrative; (b) demonstrate the need for repentance in the form of almsgiving or other merciful practices; (c) provide graphic and sometimes extreme characterizations of rich and/or poor characters; (d) utilize a rhetorical structure of reversal that involves orientation, disorientation, and reorientation, and; (e) are special "L" parables that exhibit a less radical and less negative attitude toward wealth and the wealthy when compared with other material in the Gospel.

The four shared parabolic dynamics that characterize this subset of φιλάργυροι parables are logical narrative structures and strategies geared toward the persuasion of the rich to repentance, rhetorical dynamics employed within the parable to move the reader from a vision of reality that is exclusive and elitist to a vision that is inclusive, egalitarian, and associated with Jesus' preaching of the kingdom of God. Φιλάργυροι parables: (a) are fictional stories explicitly grounded in the social, political, economic, and cultural realities of human existence; (b) metaphorically propose to the imagination an alternate vision of reality associated with aspects of Jesus' proclamation of the kingdom of God; (c) challenge and subvert the established order by guiding the hearer/reader through a process of orientation, disorientation, and reorientation, and; (d) elicit new responses, value judgments, relationships, expectations, and attitudes adequate to the alternate kingdom of God vision of reality proposed.

After presenting an original translation of the parable of the Rich Man and Lazarus, I provided a brief preliminary exegetical presentation that served to articulate the parable's threefold structure of orientation / disorientation / reorientation and to illustrate by concrete example how the four parabolic dynamics achieve their purpose of persuading the rich to repentance.

In chapter 3, I summarized the socio-narratological method described by Gowler as composed of two movements, character analysis and analysis of operative cultural scripts. I examined the subset of seven φιλάργυροι parables in the Lucan Travel Narrative in an effort to discern a coherent profile of rich characters portrayed therein and additionally analyzed operative cultural scripts to discover any recurring and convergent social concerns. I likewise examined selected works from Lucian of Samosata in a similar attempt to discern a coherent profile of rich characters and convergent social concerns.

The first step in the socio-narratological method is character analysis. Two factors must be considered when evaluating characters in a narrative text: explicitness (the clarity of the message) and reliability (the trustworthiness of the speaker). The most explicit manner for character evaluation is through direct definition, that is, the overt naming or judgment of a character's traits in the narrative. However, not all direct definitions carry the same weight. Direct definitions vary on a scale of reliability from high to low depending upon the level of authority invested in the one supplying the definition. Less explicit are indirect presentations that display various qualities and traits of characters in the course of the narrative but allow the reader to make the appropriate inferences as to what extent such qualities and traits reflect a character's true identity. Indirect presentations may take the form of speech, actions, external appearance, environment, and analogy that are interwoven throughout the narrative in descending degrees of explicitness and reliability.

The second step in the socio-narratological method is analysis of relevant cultural scripts—culturally conditioned patterns of perceiving and behaving—that are integrated into the process of apprehending the narrative development of the characters in question. The social-science models of first-century Mediterranean society are indispensable in this regard, as they help illuminate operative values, social dynamics, and worldview such as honor-shame values, patron-client relations, perception of limited goods, purity-pollution boundaries, and kinship relations. Social-science models make explicit the social values, cultural dynamics, and the worldview implicit in biblical texts to which modern readers might otherwise remain oblivious.

In my analysis of rich characters in the φιλάργυροι parables, a coherent profile emerged whereby the rich are defined as either unrepentant or repentant. On the one hand, unrepentant rich characters are described as those who: (a) are normally regarded as observant members of official Judaism (10:31–32; 18:10–12); (b) nonetheless fail to compassionately assist persons in obvious and immediate need of food, shelter, clothing, and medical attention (10:31–32; 16:19–21); (c) possess and amass large quantities of food, land, and other material resources that they hoard to

Conclusion: Rhetorical Strategy

the detriment of others in need (12:16–19); (d) may be regarded as godless, seeking and celebrating their security in material wealth (12:19–20); (e) engage in exclusive banquets designed to enhance their social standing among their elite peers (14:16–20; 16:19); (f) do not give alms but employ commercial transactions and strategies that increase their wealth (14:16–20; 16:1–3), and; (g) exhibit self-righteous behaviors and attitudes before God and others with contempt for the non-observant and non-elite (15:25–30; 18:11–12).

On the other hand, repentant rich characters are described as those who: (a) are normally regarded as non-observant Jews or non-Jews (10:33; 18:13); (b) take compassionate concrete actions to assist persons in obvious and immediate need of food, shelter, clothing, and medical attention (10:33–35); (c) engage in inclusive banquets designed to enhance their social standing among the non-elite (14:21–24); (d) employ almsgiving and other strategies that redistribute wealth to those in need (14:21–24; 16:5–7), and; (e) exhibit humble behaviors and attitudes appealing for forgiveness and mercy from God and others (15:21; 18:13).

Next, my analysis of the operative cultural scripts in the φιλάργυροι parables highlighted several recurring and convergent social concerns emphasized by Jesus as the reliable narrator of these parables and by the Lucan narrator through the placement of the parable within its immediate narrative framework. These social concerns include: (a) Jesus' reframing of the law regarding love of neighbor from one of obligations delimited by social identity to one of obligations identified by needs-based mercy and, concomitantly, the reframing of honor status as determined no longer by ascription but by performance of mercy towards those in need (10:30–35); (b) the condemnation of greed and the accumulation of wealth by the rich as forms of negative reciprocity that extract limited resources from the poor who need them to live (12:16–20); (c) the condemnation of table fellowship as a means of maintaining or enhancing honor status among the rich elite over and against the non-elite poor in displays of conspicuous consumption through balanced reciprocity and thus the exhortation to practice generalized reciprocity that benefits the poorest of the poor (14:16–24); (d) the advancement of the institution of family and kinship as the model for repentance and reconciliation among all children of God the Father, such that exclusivity and self-righteousness have no place (15:11–32); (e) an exhortation to wealthy disciples who are called to demonstrate repentance through the practice of almsgiving benefiting the poor as acts of generalized reciprocity that will accrue to righteousness at the resurrection of the just (16:1–8), and; (f) the assertion that self-righteousness leads to exclusivist attitudes and behaviors that are radically opposed to the compassionate and inclusive teaching ministry of Jesus (18:10–14).

Finally, my brief survey of selected works from Lucian of Samosata likewise yielded a coherent profile of rich characters and convergent social concerns. Rich characters are described in unequivocally negative terms as having accumulated their great wealth through outright theft and murder. Their obsession with wealth and the luxurious lifestyle fills them with pride and affords them the ability to engage in various hedonistic pursuits that include lavish dinner parties and unrestrained sexual immorality. The principal social concern expressed in these works is the extreme and apparently unbridgeable socio-economic divide between the rich and the poor. The poor are helpless before the tyranny of the rich who suffer no juridical consequences in their lifetime and behave as if they are exempt from judgment in the afterlife.

In chapter 4, I performed a detailed socio-narratological exegesis of the parable of the Rich Man and Lazarus, integrating the insights gained from my third chapter about the profile of the rich characters and convergent social concerns from the brief analyses of the other φιλάργυροι parables and the selected works of Lucian. Luke 16:14–18 serves as a prologue to the parable of the Rich Man and Lazarus, explicitly identifying the Pharisees as φιλάργυροι. In so doing, the Lucan narrator prepares the reader to make connections between the Pharisees of the narrative and the rich man of the parable. Various elements from the profile of unrepentant rich characters gleaned from the other φιλάργυροι parables are relevant for how the reader perceives the Pharisees in these verses: they are normally regarded as observant members of official Judaism; they are nonetheless godless, seeking and celebrating their security in material wealth, and; they exhibit self-righteous behaviors and attitudes before God and others with contempt for the non-observant and non-elite. The primary social concern these verses share with the other φιλάργυροι parables is that self-righteousness leads to exclusivist attitudes and behaviors that are radically opposed to the compassionate and inclusive teaching ministry of Jesus.

In its first movement (16:19–21), the parable of the Rich Man and Lazarus begins by first orienting the reader to established social, political, economic, and cultural human realities by narrating the extreme contrast in the earthly lives of the two primary characters. Each character is defined

Conclusion: Rhetorical Strategy

directly and indirectly by Jesus, the reliable narrator of the parable. The point of departure is the direct definition of the characters as rich and poor, definitions that are not simple objective descriptors but are stereotypical terms encoded with socio-narratological content from the first-century Mediterranean worldview of limited goods and from their particular use within the Lucan narrative. Each character is further defined indirectly by his actions, external appearance, and environment, resulting in a decidedly hyperbolic depiction of human reality.

In the parable's second movement (16:22–23), the reader is disoriented by the imaginative shock created by the juxtaposition in narrative form of two different visions of reality, the actual established order and a potential alternate vision. Whereas in the parable's first movement describing earthly life the rich man is blessed with prosperity and the poor man is cursed with suffering in accordance with the Deuteronomistic theological perspective, in the parable's second movement the near simultaneous deaths of the rich and poor man are narrated according to the same parallel structure as the description of their earthly lives, but in reverse order and in counterintuitive fashion. The disorientation is oxymoronic. The normally expected outcome regarding the respective fates of the rich man and poor man upon death are directly opposed to the established view of reality: in the afterlife, the allegedly cursed poor man is blessed and the presumably blessed rich man is cursed.

In the parable's third and final movement (16:24–31), the reader is re-oriented to an alternate vision of reality. Objective reality is viewed from an alternate perspective, one associated with dimensions of Jesus' proclamation of the kingdom of God. The parable depicts characters that must conform to new criteria for value judgments and human relationships—such as criteria based upon compassionate concrete actions to assist persons in obvious and immediate need of food, shelter, clothing, and medical attention as generally prescribed in Moses and the prophets. The parable demonstrates that those who fail to conform to the new criteria in the alternate vision of reality are doomed to exclusion and condemnation.

In the parable of the Rich Man and Lazarus, the rich man struggles mightily against conforming to the alternate vision of reality since he benefitted from the previously established order, value judgments, and matrix of human relationships. The existential struggle is narrated in the form of an extended dialogue between the rich man and the patriarch Abraham. The implied presumption in the third movement of the parable, then, is that the established reality is in some way defective and requires challenge and subversion in order to conform more closely to the divinely ordained order encapsulated by the symbol of the kingdom of God. Each request-denial exchange between the rich man and Abraham further demonstrates defective aspects in the rich man's character and the permanency of the new state of affairs in the afterlife.

PERSUADING THE RICH TO REPENT IN THE ΦΙΛΆΡΓΥΡΟΙ PARABLES

The seven φιλάργυροι parables of the Lucan Travel Narrative function together by utilizing a coherent rhetorical strategy of orientation, disorientation, and reorientation in an attempt to persuade the rich to repent. Recall that the fourth shared parabolic dynamic among the φιλάργυροι parables is that they elicit new responses, value judgments, relationships, expectations, and attitudes adequate to the alternate kingdom of God vision of reality proposed. This final section will briefly explore two such responses adequate to the alternate kingdom of God vision of reality proposed: the proper use of wealth and proper social relations in Christian discipleship.

Proper Use of Wealth in Christian Discipleship

Most of the seven φιλάργυροι parables orient readers to the reality wherein the rich elite practice forms of balanced or negative reciprocity. As we have seen, balanced reciprocity refers to interactions in which the interests and needs of both parties are addressed. The rendering of equivalent benefits is insured by keeping track of the quantity and quality of the goods and services exchanged. Balanced reciprocity governs relations among neighbors and in the marketplace.[12] Such balanced reciprocity is depicted, for example, in the parable of the Great Banquet (Luke 14:16–24) where the rich host originally invited his fellow rich elite to exclusive table fellowship in a bid to enhance, or at least maintain, his elite honor status and affiliation. The implicit understanding is that he would be invited to such elite table fellowship in the future, with the result that the material and instrumental resources of food and honor circulate more or less equally in the upper echelons of society.

---

12. Neyrey, "Ceremonies," 371–73.

Negative reciprocity, however, refers to one party extracting something from another without any intention for reciprocation, essentially covering theft, robbery, and all forms of forced expropriation of another's goods and services. Such negative reciprocity would be practiced only on those perceived as outsiders, strangers, or enemies.[13] Negative reciprocity is depicted, for example, in the parables of the Rich Fool and the Rich Man and Lazarus where the men accumulate and hoard food needed by others for their very survival.

The φιλάργυροι parables attempt to persuade the rich to repent of these sanctioned economic policies of balanced and negative reciprocity and to embrace instead the policy of generalized reciprocity as practiced within the alternate kingdom of God vision of reality. Generalized reciprocity refers to assistance, whether financial, material, or influential, that focuses immediately on the interests and needs of another party. While the expectation of returned assistance is always implied, it is left indefinite and open-ended. Some forms of generalized reciprocity include hospitality and gifts and are characteristic of the kind of assistance among family members and kin.[14] The kind of repentance envisioned is one that embraces generalized reciprocity as it is depicted, for example, in the parables of the Good Samaritan and the Great Banquet, providing immediate assistance to persons in need of food, shelter, and medical attention. It is important to note that the φιλάργυροι parables do not advocate the complete divestiture of wealth but rather its more equitable distribution among those most in need.

Proper Social Relations in Christian Discipleship

In a similar fashion, most of the seven φιλάργυροι parables orient readers to the reality of patron-client relations. While inherently unequal in power, the patron-client relationship is mutually beneficial on several counts. Patrons have instrumental, economic, and political resources (food, money, material resources, influence) and can offer clients needed support and protection. Clients, in exchange, can offer intangible resources such as respect, reputation, and enduring loyalty and provide an outlet for public expressions of generosity that enhance the patron's honor. There is a strong element of solidarity in such patron-client relations, linked to the mutually

13. Ibid.
14. Ibid.

beneficial exchange of needed resources and associated with maintaining personal honor and obligations.[15]

Most of the φιλάργυροι parables depict rich patrons who consistently fail to fulfill their social and religious obligations toward needy clients. It is important to note, however, that these parables do not advocate a simple return to the patron-client system. Rather, the alternate kingdom of God vision of reality demands that social relations among persons be characterized by the kind of relationships that characterize families and kin, regardless of social status or economic condition.

In the final analysis, the rich of the world who remain stubbornly unrepentant in their earthly life despite Jesus' proclamation of the alternate kingdom of God vision of reality will indubitably share the terrifying fate of the anonymous rich men of the φιλάργυροι parables in the afterlife: they will be tormented in Hades forevermore.

---

15. Eisenstadt and Roniger, *Patrons, Clients and Friends*, 48–49.

Bibliography

Primary Sources

The Gospel of Thomas: The Hidden Sayings of Jesus. Translated by M. Meyer. San Francisco: Harper, 1992.

Lucian. Translated by A. M. Harmon. 8 vols.: New York: Putnam's Sons, 1929. *Cataplus* 2.1–57; *Gallus* 2.171–239; *De Luctu* 4.111–31.

Nestle, E., and K. Aland, editors. *Novum Testamentum Graece*: 27th rev. ed. Stuttgart: Deutsche Bibelgesellschaft, 2001.

Palestinian Talmud (*y. Sanh.* 6.6 23c, 30–41.42–43 and *y. Hag.* 2.2 77d, 42–54.54–57).

S. Aurelii Augustini Hipponensis Episcopi. "Quaestionum Evangeliorum Libri Duo." *Patrologia Latina*, vol. 35, edited by J.-P. Migne, 1350–52. Paris: Migne, 1844–64.

Secondary Sources

Aalen, Sverre. "St. Luke's Gospel and the Last Chapters of *I Enoch*." *NTS* 13 (1966–67) 1–13.

Bailey, Kenneth E. *Jesus through Middle Eastern Eyes: Cultural Studies in the Gospels*. Downers Grove, IL: InterVarsity, 2008.

———. *Poet and Peasant: A Literary Cultural Approach to the Parables in Luke*. Grand Rapids: Eerdmans, 1976.

Ball, Michael. "The Parables of the Unjust Steward and the Rich Man and Lazarus." *ExpTim* 106 (1995) 329–30.

Ballard, P. H. "Reasons for Refusing the Great Supper." *JTS* 23 (1972) 341–50.

Bauckham, Richard J. "Descent to the Underworld." In *ABD*, vol. 2, edited by D. N. Freedman et al., 145–59. New York: Doubleday, 1992.

———. "The Rich Man and Lazarus: The Parable and the Parallels." *NTS* 37 (1991) 225–46.

———. "The Rich Man and Lazarus: The Parable and the Parallels." In *The Fate of the Dead: Studies on the Jewish and Christian Apocalypses*, 97–118. NovTSup 93. Leiden: Brill, 1998.

———. "Visiting the Places of the Dead in the Extra-Canonical Apocalyses." In *The Fate of the Dead: Studies on the Jewish and Christian Apocalypses*, 81–96. NovTSup 93. Leiden: Brill, 1998.

Bibliography

Berger, Peter L. *The Sacred Canopy: Elements of a Sociological Theory of Religion*. New York: Doubleday, 1990.

Berger, Peter L., and Thomas Luckmann. *The Social Construction of Reality: A Treatise in the Sociology of Knowledge*. New York: Doubleday, 1989.

Black, Max. *Models and Metaphors: Studies in Language and Philosophy*. Ithaca, NY: Cornell University Press, 1962.

Bock, Darrell L. *Luke*. Baker Exegetical Commentary on the New Testament. Grand Rapids: Baker Academic, 1996.

Boring, M. Eugene, Klaus Berger, and Carsten Colpe, editors. *Hellenistic Commentary to the New Testament*. Nashville: Abingdon, 1995.

Braun, Willi. *Feasting and Social Rhetoric in Luke 14*. Edited by M. Thrall. SNTSMS 85. Cambridge: Cambridge University Press, 1995.

Bretherton, D. J. "Lazarus of Bethany: Resurrection or Resuscitation?" *ExpTim* 104 (1993) 169–73.

Brown, Raymond E. "Parable and Allegory Reconsidered." *NovT* 5 (1962) 36–45.

Brown, Raymond E., and Sandra M. Schneiders. "Hermeneutics." *NJBC* 1146–65.

Bultmann, Rudolf. *Die Geschichte der synoptischen Tradition*. 2nd ed. Göttingen: Vandenhoeck & Ruprecht, 1931.

Burghardt, Walter. "On Early Christian Exegesis." *TS* 11 (1950) 78–116.

Crossan, John Dominic. *In Parables: The Challenge of the Historical Jesus*. San Francisco: Harper & Row, 1973.

Darr, John A. *On Character Building: The Reader and the Rhetoric of Characterization in Luke-Acts*. Literary Currents in Biblical Interpretation. Louisville: Westminster/John Knox, 1992.

Derrett, J. Duncan M. "Fresh Light on St. Luke XVI: The Parable of the Unjust Steward." *NTS* 7 (1960–61) 198–219.

———. *Law in the New Testament*. London: Darton, Longman & Todd, 1970.

Donahue, John R. *The Gospel in Parable: Metaphor, Narrative, and Theology in the Synoptic Gospels*. Philadelphia: Fortress, 1988.

Donald, T. "The Semantic Field of 'Folly' in Proverbs, Job, Psalms, and Ecclesiastes." *VT* 13 (1963) 285–92.

Drury, John. *The Parables in the Gospels: History and Allegory*. New York: Crossroad, 1985.

Eisenstadt, S. N., and Luis Roniger. *Patrons, Clients and Friends: Interpersonal Relations and the Structure of Trust in Society*. Cambridge: Cambridge University Press, 1984.

Elliott, John H. "Temple Versus Household in Luke-Acts: A Contrast in Social Institutions." In *The Social World of Luke-Acts: Models for Interpretation*, edited by J. H. Neyrey, 211–40. Peabody, MA: Hendrickson, 1991.

Ewen, Yosef. "The Theory of Character in Narrative Fiction." *Hasifrut* 3 (1971) 1–30.

Fitzmyer, Joseph A. *The Gospel according to Luke*. 2 vols. AB 28–28a. New York: Doubleday, 1981, 1985.

Forster, E. M. *Aspects of the Novel*. New York: Penguin, 1962.

Funk, Robert W. *Language, Hermeneutic, and the Word of God: The Problem of Language in the New Testament and Contemporary Theology*. New York: Harper & Row, 1966.

Gowler, David B. "Characterization in Luke: A Socio-Narratological Approach." *BTB* 19 (1989) 54–62.

———. *Host, Guest, Enemy and Friend: Portraits of the Pharisees in Luke and Acts*. 1991. Reprint. Eugene, OR: Wipf & Stock, 2008.

———. *What Are They Saying About the Parables?* New York: Paulist, 2000.

Bibliography

Green, Joel B. *The Gospel of Luke*. Grand Rapids: Eerdmans, 1997.
Grensted, L. W. "The Use of *Enoch* in St. Luke xvi. 19–31." *ExpTim* 26 (1914–15) 333–34.
Gressmann, Hugo. *Vom reichen Mann und armen Lazarus: Eine literargeschichtliche Studie*. AKPAW phil.-hist. Kl. 7; Berlin: Konigliche Akademie der Wissenschaften, 1918.
Griffith, Francis Llewellyn. *Stories of the High Priests of Memphis: The Sethon of Herodotus and the Demotic Tales of Khamuas*. Oxford: Clarendon, 1900.
Grobel, K. "'. . . Whose Name Was Neves.'" *NTS* 10 (1964) 373–82.
Guillet, J. "Les exégètes d'Alexandrie et d'Antioche: Conflit ou malentenu?" *RSR* 34 (1947) 257–302.
Harvey, W. J. *Character and the Novel*. Ithaca, NY: Cornell University Press, 1966.
Heil, John Paul. *The Meal Scenes in Luke-Acts: An Audience-Oriented Approach*. SBLMS 52. Atlanta: Society of Biblical Literature, 1999.
Herzog, William R. *Parables as Subversive Speech: Jesus as Pedagogue of the Oppressed*. Louisville: Westminster/John Knox, 1994.
Hesse, Mary. *Models and Analogies in Science*. South Bend, IN: Notre Dame University Press, 1966.
Himmelfarb, Martha. *Ascent to Heaven in Jewish and Christian Apocalypses*. New York: Oxford University Press, 1993.
———. *Tours of Hell: An Apocalyptic Form in Jewish and Christian Literature*. Philadelphia: University of Pennsylvania Press, 1983.
Hochman, Baruch. *Character in Literature*. New York: Cornell University Press, 1985.
Hock, Ronald F. "Lazarus and Micyllus: Greco-Roman Backgrounds to Luke 16:19–31." *JBL* 106 (1987) 447–63.
Hultgren, Arland J. *The Parables of Jesus: A Commentary*. Grand Rapids: Eerdmans, 2000.
Jeremias, Joachim. *The Parables of Jesus*. [1947] Translated by S. H. Hooke. 2nd rev. ed. Upper Saddle River, NJ: Prentice-Hall, 1963.
Johnson, Luke Timothy. *The Gospel of Luke*. SP 3. Collegeville, MN: Liturgical, 1991.
———. *The Literary Function of Possessions in Luke-Acts*. SBLDS 39. Missoula, MT: Scholars, 1977.
———. *Sharing Possessions: Mandate and Symbol of Faith*. OBT. Philadelphia: Fortress, 1981.
Jülicher, Adolf. *Die Gleichnisreden Jesu*. 2 vols. Freiburg: Mohr Siebeck, 1888, 1889. Reprinted in one volume Darmstadt: Wissenschaftliche Buchgesellschaft, 1969.
Lehtipuu, Outi. *The Afterlife Imagery in Luke's Story of the Rich Man and Lazarus*. NovTSup 123. Leiden: Brill, 2007.
———. "Characterization and Persuasion: The Rich Man and the Poor Man in Luke 16.19–31." In *Characterization in the Gospel: Reconceiving Narrative Criticism*, edited by D. Rhoads and K. Syreeni, 73–105. JSNTSup 184. Sheffield, UK: Sheffield Academic Press, 1999.
Lévi, Israel. "Un Recueil des contes Juifs inédits." *REJ* 35 (1897) 65–83.
Lichtheim, Miriam. *Ancient Egyptian Literature: A Book of Reading: The Late Period*. Berkeley: University of California Press, 1980.
Malina, Bruce J. *The New Testament World: Insights from Cultural Anthropology*. Rev. ed. Louisville: Westminster/John Knox, 1993.
———. *The Social Gospel of Jesus: The Kingdom of God in Mediterranean Perspective*. Minneapolis: Fortress, 2001.
———. "Wealth and Poverty in the New Testament and Its World." *Int* 41 (1987) 354–67.

Bibliography

Malina, Bruce J., and Jerome H. Neyrey. "Honor and Shame in Luke-Acts: Pivotal Values of the Mediterranean World." In *The Social World of Luke-Acts: Models for Interpretation*, edited by J. H. Neyrey, 25-65. Peabody, MA: Hendrickson, 1991.

Malina, Bruce J., and Richard L. Rohrbaugh. *Social Science Commentary on the Synoptic Gospels*. Minneapolis: Fortress, 1992.

Marshall, I. Howard. *The Gospel of Luke: A Commentary on the Greek Text*. NIGTC 3. Exeter, UK: Paternoster, 1978.

Maspero, Gaston. "Contes relatives aux grands prêtres de Memphis." *Journal des savants* (1901) 473-504.

———. *Popular Stories of Ancient Egypt*. Translated by A. S. Johns. New Hyde Park, NY: University, 1967.

Matera, Frank J. "Jesus' Journey to Jerusalem (Luke 9.51—19.46): A Conflict with Israel." *JSNT* 51 (1993) 57-77.

Metzger, Bruce M. *A Textual Commentary on the Greek New Testament*. 2nd ed. Stuttgart: Deutsche Bibelgesellschaft, 1994.

Metzger, James A. *Consumption and Wealth in Luke's Travel Narrative*. BIS 88. Leiden: Brill, 2007.

Moxnes, Halvor. *The Economy of the Kingdom: Social Conflict and Economic Relations in Luke's Gospel*. OBT. Philadelphia: Fortress, 1988.

———. "Patron-Client Relations and the New Community in Luke-Acts." In *The Social World of Luke-Acts: Models for Interpretation*, edited by J. H. Neyrey, 241-68. Peabody, MA: Hendrickson, 1991.

Neyrey, Jerome H. "Ceremonies in Luke-Acts: The Case of Meals and Table Fellowship." In *The Social World of Luke-Acts: Models for Interpretation*, edited by J. H. Neyrey. 361-87. Peabody, MA: Hendrickson, 1991.

———. "The Symbolic Universe of Luke-Acts: 'They Turn The World Upside Down.'" In *The Social World of Luke-Acts: Models for Interpretation*, edited by J. H. Neyrey, 271-304. Peabody, MA: Hendrickson, 1991.

Nickelsburg, George W. E. *1 Enoch 1: A Commentary on the Book of 1 Enoch, Chapters 1-36; 81-108*. Hermeneia. Minneapolis: Fortress, 2001.

———. "The Apocalyptic Message of 1 Enoch 92-105." *CBQ* 39 (1977) 309-28.

———. "Revisiting the Rich and Poor in *1 Enoch* 92-105 and the Gospel according to Luke." *SBLSP* 37 (1998) 579-605.

———. "Riches, the Rich and God's Judgment in *1 Enoch* 92-105 and the Gospel according to Luke." *NTS* 25 (1979) 324-44.

Nolland, John. *Luke*. 3 vols. WBC 35. Nashville: Thomas Nelson, 1989, 1993.

Oakman, Douglas E. "The Ancient Economy in the Bible." *BTB* 21 (1991) 34-39.

———. *Jesus and the Economic Questions of His Day*. Lewiston, NY: Mellen, 1986.

———. "Was Jesus a Peasant? Implications for Reading the Samaritan Story (Luke 10:30-35)." *BTB* 22 (1992) 117-25.

Paffenroth, Kim. *The Story of Jesus according to L*. JSNTSup 147. Sheffield, UK: Sheffield Academic Press, 1997.

Perrin, Norman. *Jesus and the Language of the Kingdom: Symbol and Metaphor in New Testament Interpretation*. Philadelphia: Fortress, 1976.

Ricoeur, Paul. "Biblical Hermeneutics." *Semeia* 4 (1975) 122-28.

———. *The Rule of Metaphor: Multi-Disciplinary Studies in the Creation of Meaning in Language*. Translated by R. Czerny. Toronto: University of Toronto Press, 1981.

Bibliography

Rimmon-Kenan, Shlomith. *Narrative Fiction: Contemporary Poetics*. London: Routledge, 1983.

Robinson, Maurice A. "The Rich Man and Lazarus—Luke 16:19–31: Text-Critical Notes." In *Translating the New Testament: Text, Translation, Theology*, edited by S. E. Porter and M. J. Boda, 96–110. Grand Rapids: Eerdmans, 2009.

Roth, Catharine P., Translator. *St. John Chrysostom: On Wealth and Poverty*. Crestwood, NY: St. Vladimir's Seminary Press, 1984.

Sanders, Jack T. *The Jews in Luke-Acts*. Philadelphia: Fortress, 1987.

Sandmel, Samuel. "Parellelomania." *JBL* 81 (1962) 1–13.

Scott, Bernard Brandon. *Hear Then the Parable: A Commentary on the Parables of Jesus*. Minneapolis: Fortress, 1989.

Snodgrass, Klyne R. *Stories with Intent: A Comprehensive Guide to the Parables of Jesus*. Grand Rapids: Eerdmans, 2008.

Standen, A. O. "The Parable of Dives and Lazarus and Enoch 22." *ExpTim* 33 (1921–22) 523.

Talbert, Charles. *Literary Patterns, Theological Themes, and the Genre of Luke-Acts*. SBLMS 20. Missoula, MT: Scholars, 1974.

Tannehill, Robert C. *Luke*. ANTC. Nashville: Abingdon, 1996.

———. *The Narrative Unity of Luke-Acts: A Literary Interpretation*. 2 vols. Philadelphia: Fortress, 1986, 1990.

Wailes, Stephen L. *Medieval Allegories of Jesus' Parables*. Berkeley: University of California Press, 1987.

Wheelwright, Philip. *Metaphor and Reality*. Bloomington, IN: Indiana University Press, 1962.

Scripture Citations

OLD TESTAMENT

Genesis
5:24	65, 138
12:1–3	66, 142

Exodus
6:23	131
9–11	132

Leviticus
19:18	41, 102

Numbers
25:7, 11	59

Deuteronomy
6:5	102
7:25	123
12:31	123
14:28–29	143
18:12	123
20:5–7	106
24:1–4	126
24:5	106
27:15	123
28	134
28:35	132
29:17	123
32:16	123

Joshua
18:17	88

Judges
8:26	132

1 Samuel
2:1–10	71
16:7	123
28:6–19	61
28:7–20	67, 143

1 Kings
1:21	65, 138
2:10	65, 138
8:39	123
11:21	65, 138
14:11	64, 133
16:4	64, 133
21:24	64, 133

2 Kings
2:11	65, 138
21:6	61, 67, 143

1 Chronicles
28:9	123

Esther

8:15	132

Job

31:24–28	89

Psalms

7:10	123
14:1	89
21:8	123
34:16	123
53:1	89

Proverbs

21:2	123
24:12	123

Ecclesiastes

2:1–11	89

Isaiah

2:8, 20	123
8:19	61, 67, 143
10:1–4	143
17:8	123
22:13	90
41:24	123
44:19	123
58:5–7	143
61	71

Jeremiah

7:5–6	143

Amos

8:4–6	143

Zechariah

7:9–10	143

APOCRYPHA

Wisdom

1–5	14
2:6	14
3:1	14
3:2	14
3:5	14
3:13, 18	14
4:7	14
4:19	14
5:3	14
5:4	14
5:6	14
5:8	14

Sirach

11:18–19	89
11:19	90

2 Esdras

7:106	142
8:56–59	144

4 Maccabees

13:17	65, 138

PSEUDEPIGRAPHA

1 Enoch

1–36	14
18:11–16	146
21:1–10	146
22	13, 14, 139
22:1–14	146
37–71	14
72–82	14
83–90	14
91	14
92–105	14, 139
96:4–8	16
97:8–10	43
99:2	15
104:9	15
106–7	14

108	14

4 Ezra

7:74–101	139

NEW TESTAMENT

Mark

4:13–20	3
10:11–12	126
10:17–22	70

Matthew

5:3	71
5:6	71
5:31–32	126
8:6, 14	133
9:2	133
13:36–43	3
15:27	60
19:8–9	126
19:16–22	70

Luke

1:6	86
1:10–20	86
1:46–55	21, 71
1:50–55	143
1:51–53	71
1:51	123
1:53	89
1:67–79	87
1:73	66, 142
2:8	89
2:48	66, 144
3–19	24, 40
3:1	89
3:7–14	28
3:8, 10–11	21
3:8	41
3:8, 10	142
3:12	98, 111
4:12	102
4:16–21	20, 126
4:16–19	25
4:18–19	71
4:18	130
5:11, 28	20
5:21–22	90
5:22	123
5:27—6:5	27
5:27–32	111
5:29–32	108
5:29	105
6	67
6:8	90
6:17–49	102
6:17–19	21
6:20–26	21, 28, 143
6:20–22	130
6:20	71
6:21	64, 71
6:24–25	72
6:24	89
6:32–36	104
6:45	123
7:13	87, 95
7:16–17	21
7:18–23	126
7:22	130
7:29–30	45, 98, 108, 122, 125
7:29, 34	111
7:30	20, 41
7:34	108
7:36–50	27, 108
7:38, 45	95
7:40–43	24, 40
8:26	89
8:27	132
9:1–6	20
9:17	64
9:20	20
9:45	20
9:46	20
9:47	123
9:51—19:46	69
9:52–53	87
10:13–15	66, 138
10:25	41
10:27	123
10:29	41
10:30–37a	24, 40
10:30–35	40, 41, 72, 86, 102, 151, 153

Luke *(cont.)*

10:30	63, 64
10:31–32	87, 152
10:31	86
10:32	86
10:33–35	153
10:33–34	42
10:33	86, 87, 95, 153
10:34–35	88
10:35	87
10:36–37	41
11:1–13	108
11:5b–8	24, 40
11:14–16, 23	21
11:27–28	105
11:29–32	42
11:37–54	27
11:37–52	107
11:37–44	108
11:39–44	125
11:39–42	47
11:39	98, 111, 122, 127
11:40	89, 98, 111
11:42	98, 111
11:46	102
11:47	102
11:52	102
12	32
12:1	20, 98, 111
12:1b—13:9	43
12:13–15, 21	42
12:16–21	25
12:16–20	40, 42, 43, 72, 89, 104, 151, 153
12:16–19	153
12:15–21	14
12:16	63, 89, 96
12:16b–20	24, 40
12:19–20	153
12:17–19	89
12:19	43, 90, 105, 108, 131
12:20	89
12:22–34	108
12:34	123
12:42	96
12:56	43
13:6b–9	24, 40
13:10–17b	24
14	31
14:1–24	27, 107
14:1–7	108
14:1	105
14:1, 3	43
14:2, 16	63
14:11	20, 123
14:12–14	33, 107, 143
14:12–13	92
14:13–14	110
14:13, 21	130
14:15	105
14:16–24	40, 43, 72, 91, 105, 151, 153, 156
14:16–20	153
14:16	91, 131
14:18	91
14:19	91
14:20	92
14:21–24	153
14:21–23	91
14:21	91, 92
14:23	92
14:28–32	24, 40
15	31
15:1–32	27
15:1–2	111, 124
15:1	98, 124, 127
15:2	44, 107, 109, 123
15:3–32	108, 124
15:4–6	24, 40
15:7	45, 94
15:7, 10	108
15:8–9	24, 40
15:10	45, 94
15:11–32	3, 24, 25, 40, 44, 72, 93, 107, 151, 153
15:11	63
15:13–15	89
15:16	60, 64, 131
15:17–19	93
15:18–19	45
15:20	87, 95
15:21	153
15:23–24	90, 94, 131
15:24, 32	108

Scripture Citations

15:25–30	153	16:21	60, 133, 137
15:29–30	45, 94, 109	16:21b	64
15:29, 32	90, 131	16:22–24	2
15:31	95	16:22–23	65, 136–37, 155
15:32	95, 108	16:22	60, 65
16	32, 69, 121	16:23	60, 65
16:1–13	25, 123	16:24–31	66, 140–41, 155
16:1–9	69, 124	16:24–26	2, 142
16:1–8	40, 45, 72, 96, 110, 151, 154	16:24	66, 145
		16:24, 25	66, 144
16:1–3	153	16:24, 27, 30	142
16:1	96	16:25–26	66, 67
16:1, 19	63	16:25	12, 66, 72, 142
16:1b–8a	24, 40	16:26–31	6
16:2	96	16:26	6, 67, 143, 146
16:3	96, 97	16:27–31	2, 8, 68
16:4	97	16:27–29	143
16:5–7	153	16:27–28	66, 67
16:6	97	16:29	66, 67
16:7	98	16:30–31	143
16:8	96, 97, 110	16:30	60, 61, 66, 68
16:9	110	16:31	15, 61, 66, 68
16:10–13	69, 124	17:7–10	24, 40
16:9–12	46	17:15–16	87
16:9	69, 122	17:20, 22	111
16:13	31, 46, 72	18:2–8a	24, 40
16:13, 14	123	18:9–14	108, 127
16:14–18	120, 128, 154	18:9	47, 111
16:14–15	69, 121, 122	18:10–14	40, 47, 72, 98, 111, 151, 154
16:14	20, 31, 40, 46, 47, 122, 123, 124	18:10–14a	24, 40
		18:10–12	152
16:15–18	127	18:10	98
16:15, 18	98, 111	18:11–12	153
16:15	20, 102, 122, 125	18:11	99
16:15a	122	18:13	99, 153
16:15b	123	18:14	20, 23
16:16–18	47, 69, 121, 125	18:15	23
16:18	126	18:18–23	26, 70
16:19–31	ix, 1, 4, 14, 24, 25, 27, 39, 40, 43, 46, 57–59, 62, 69, 72, 120, 148, 151, 152	18:18	26
		18:22	26
		18:28	20
16:19–26	6, 8, 10	18:34	20
16:19–25	6	19:1–10	26, 27, 70, 107
16:19–21	2, 63, 129–30, 133, 154	19:2–10	24
16:19	59, 63, 90, 96, 130, 153	19:5–7	108
		19:8	26
16:20–21a	64	19:9	26
16:20	63, 130	19:10	23

169

Luke (cont.)

19:12	63
19:27	23
19:44	23
20:9	63
20:14	90
21:21	89
22:24	20
22:60–62	21
23:35	123
24	68

John

1:18	66, 138
11	64
13:23	65, 138

Acts of the Apostles

8:1	89
9:33	63
10:17	133
10:39	89
12:13–14	133
12:20	89
13:49	89
14:13	133
16:6	89
18:23	89
20:38	66, 144
26:20	89
27:27	89

1 Corinthians

7:10–11	126
15:32	90

1 Thessalonians

2:4–7a	121

1 Timothy

6:2b–16	121
6:10	121

2 Timothy

2:14—3:17	121

Titus

1:7–11	121

Revelation

2:22	133
16:2	132
18:11–17	132

EARLY CHRISTIAN WRITINGS

Gospel of Thomas

63	89
64	91

www.ingramcontent.com/pod-product-compliance
Lightning Source LLC
Chambersburg PA
CBHW071457150426
43191CB00008B/1372